NAME

START DATE

END DATE

CONTENTS

One Step Closer
DEVOTIONAL GUIDE
From Worrier
to Warrior
CANDACE CAMERON BURE

A NOTE FROM CANDACE

INTRODUCTION

Even if you've never stepped foot inside a church, everyone seems to know the story of David and Goliath. It's from the Bible, and it's often referenced when an underdog in business or sports or the schoolyard goes up against the favored.

David's opponent wasn't just an allegory. He was a living legend—a champion among his people, the ancient Philistines. Based on reported historical measurements, scholars believe Goliath was nearly ten feet tall. When it comes to worry, fear, or anxiety, these are ten-foot-tall giants that aren't so easy to spot. Our thoughts can freeze us, leaving us unable to live the full lives that God has for us. Worry is personal—and spiritual. It can crush the children of God and hinder the kingdom of God (which is exactly what our enemy is trying to do).

From my own life, and the stories of others, I'm convinced that worry is a sneaky intruder that enters through the back door. Fear is happy to bust through the front door, setting off alarms and stirring up panic. Worry? It's fear in stealth mode. Way quieter, but just as destructive. Worry eats away at a woman's spirit, poking constant holes in her courage, nitpicking at any bit of faith that she may have built up.

Sometimes our worry is undefined; we just feel its cloud hanging over us all the time: *Is my kid okay? Do I measure up? Is another shoe about to drop? What should I do with my life?* Sometimes, though, it's very specific:

How will I pay my bills this month?

Can my friend forgive me?

What does the boss think of me? (or my man? or my Instagram followers?)

Will my sick parent ever get better?

Should I get out of this relationship?

What if I fail at this goal?

How do I fix this problem?

Will I ever fit in with these people?

With its constant nagging, worry weakens us by the day. That's why we have to fight it day after day.

You may be saying, "I wish it was that easy, Candace."

Friend, I know it's not. It's not for me either. Yet I've seen that we women can be as brave as anybody once we're clear on what God says and supplies. As soon as we start to find our strength in Him and His Word, things change. Worry fades, and faith takes charge.

How about if we fight worry for thirty days—together? Whether you need to spread out that process over several weeks or you decide to do it for thirty days straight, let's team up and grow from worriers to warriors! If we can develop a new habit in twenty-one days (that's what the experts say), then I know we can renew our minds, build up our faith, and gain a new level of confidence in thirty!

To get us *One Step Closer* to that goal of becoming the warriors we've been created to be, my friends at DaySpring and I have packed thirty days' worth of "mission support" inside these pages. That means *no worries for you*! There's no seminary degree or church background required to join me. You don't even have to own a Bible. Just bring along something to write with and a willing spirit, and you're covered. This devotional guide is equipped with all the basic gear for building courage and winning the war: the power of Scripture, a devotional reading from my heart to yours, guided questions where you and I can clarify our struggles with worry, and lots of creative exercises for taking action to win! Together we will learn to protect our thoughts and guard our hearts. The more we can focus our eyes and minds on the truths of God, the less power worry will have in our lives.

God says in the Bible that He fights for those who trust in Him. By following His lead and putting our faith in Him, we win, because He wins! His uplifting truths encourage us, and His everlasting love cheers us on, as we move one step closer to seeing differently, thinking differently, and believing differently.

Let's start TODAY!

In this together,

Candace

QUICK Q&A FROM CANDACE

Wherever you are on your spiritual journey, I want you to know you're not alone. In this first section, I've answered some questions people typically ask me about my Christian faith. I hope these answers will be helpful to you too.

WHY SHOULD I READ AND STUDY THE BIBLE?

While the Bible is full of history, wisdom, guidelines, and poetry, it's actually the epic story about all of creation and time from the beginning to the end. In the Bible, God is the ultimate storyteller—He shares His plan, His story, and His design for the world and for humanity. No other book is so transformational because no other book shows us how much we are loved by our Creator.

WHAT DOES IT MEAN TO BE "SAVED"?

When followers of Jesus talk about being saved, we mean that Jesus rescued us from the ultimate consequence of sin—eternal separation from God. When we continually choose *our* way rather than *God's* way, we become filled with darkness, hopelessness, shame, guilt, and fear. Being "saved" means we acknowledge that Jesus is the way, and He shines His light, freedom, joy, peace, and hope into our lives.

WHAT IF I DON'T NEED TO BE "SAVED"?

I get this too—you're a good person and you're not hurting anyone. Why do you need to be "saved," right? We have to realize that God's standards are different from human standards. If we just compare ourselves to other people, it's easy to think we're good enough. But when we compare ourselves to God's standards, we fall miserably short. Every. Single. Time. But because God loves us, He sent His Son, Jesus, to die so that all people—the bad, the good, and everyone in between—could be fully forgiven in His eyes and have a loving relationship with Him.

IS THERE REALLY ONLY ONE WAY TO GOD?

This is a tough one for a lot of people, but the short answer is *yes*. There is only one way to God, and it's through Jesus Christ. Jesus said, "I am the way, the truth, and the life. No one can come to the Father except through Me" (John 14:6). Jesus didn't say, "I am one of the ways to God." He's *it*—He's the *only* way.

Though this idea may seem very narrow, it's actually comforting. Many religions teach people to work to earn their right standing with God. With Jesus, being right with God doesn't depend on what we do or don't do; it depends on what Jesus has already done: He died on the cross to take the punishment for our sins and then rose again to give us life with Him. All we have to do is acknowledge our sinfulness, ask God for His forgiveness, and then accept His gift of salvation. Then we get to spend our lives loving Him.

HOW CAN I HAVE A RELATIONSHIP WITH GOD?

If you ask God how to find Him, He will make it very clear to you. One way to strengthen your bond with your heavenly Father is simply to talk to Him—tell Him your worries, fears, concerns, doubts, hopes, dreams. Tell Him all of it! Prayer doesn't need to be long or eloquent. Physical posture or volume doesn't make prayer more or less effective. God has only one requirement for effective prayer: to "be sure that your faith is in God alone" (James 1:6).

And listen for God's voice. How do you know when God is speaking to you? God speaks to us in different ways, and He'll never say something that contradicts what the Bible teaches. When I'm reading certain verses and my heart does something like a flip-flop, I know in that moment that God is showing me something important and I need to pay attention.

God will also speak to us through friends, pastors, and teachers. He may even reveal Himself to us through nature or certain circumstances. Just be open to however He wants to speak to you.

HOW DO I USE THIS DEVOTIONAL GUIDE?

I love this devotional guide because it encourages you to experience the life-changing message of God's Word for yourself. Each of the thirty entries includes the following:

- **WHAT GOD SAYS ABOUT WORRYING**
  Each entry starts with Scripture passages that address the topics of worry, fear, and anxiety. God's Word tells us how to combat worry and embrace God's peace and joy. Be sure to read each verse, say the words out loud, and maybe even memorize these verses so you can repeat them back to yourself when you find negative thoughts dominating your mind.

- **A MESSAGE FROM ME**
  I love telling people about the many ways God has showed up in my life. My hope is that by sharing my real-life moments of how I've leaned on my Savior to get me through this life, you'll find that God wants to help you with anything at any time. He longs to take the pressure off us. It's taken me a long time to understand this (and let's face it, I still forget a lot), but it's true! He's got this!

- **REFLECTION QUESTIONS**
  Your turn! It's time to answer a few questions about where you are, how you're feeling, and who you are becoming. Sometimes the answers will come quickly, and sometimes you may have to do some soul searching, but either way, the exercise of writing it down will help you acknowledge and focus on where you are on your spiritual journey. Be honest! This is your safe place.

- **INTERACTIVE ACTIVITIES**
  I want you to think outside the box, so every entry includes a different interactive activity such as filling in a list, shading in boxes, adding to a chart—all ways to help you find a fresh, new perspective on the topic at hand.

- **QR CODES**
  Want more? I created thirty videos for you! And you have exclusive access to these. All you need to do is scan the QR code at the bottom of each entry and the videos will pop up. Here's how to open a QR code:
    1. Open the camera on your phone.
    2. Point the camera at the QR code (the small, square barcode-looking, black-and-white box in the bottom right corner). If your front-facing camera is on, first tap the camera-shaped icon to flip it.
    3. Make sure the QR code is centered on the camera screen. All four edges of the QR code should be on the screen.
    4. Wait for the code to scan. (It should scan almost immediately.)
    5. Open the QR code's content. Tap the notification that appears at the top of the screen to open the QR code's webpage or other information.

My hope is that through this thirty-day journey—through the Scripture passages, testimonies, questions, activities, and videos—you'll be able to release all your worries and fears to God and know that He is going to equip you with the strength, wisdom, power, and courage to be a warrior who can face whatever comes your way.

LET'S DO THIS!

I'm thrilled we are about to embark on this journey together. We are about to go from being worried about the things we see in front of us to being confident and secure in the fact that God sees so much more than we do. God is fighting for us, and He is going to give us everything we need to face any struggles we are currently experiencing and any hard times that might be around the corner. We can live through all of it with an inner power, an unmovable force—as strong warriors who have already won the fight.

Before we get started, let's all say this little prayer and ask God to be with us in this process.

Dear God, be with me during this thirty-day journey. I want to be closer to You, I want to trust You more, I want to live unafraid. You know, Lord, that sometimes my thoughts run away from me and I'm unable to stop them. I worry about my life, my plans, my health, my family, my friends—and the list keeps going. Help me to stop worrying and start living a fearless life, trusting You with every single person and problem in my life. Show me what I need to learn to grow closer to You, shine Your light on the topics in this book that I need to dive deeper into, and help me live a life of peace and security. In Jesus's name. Amen.

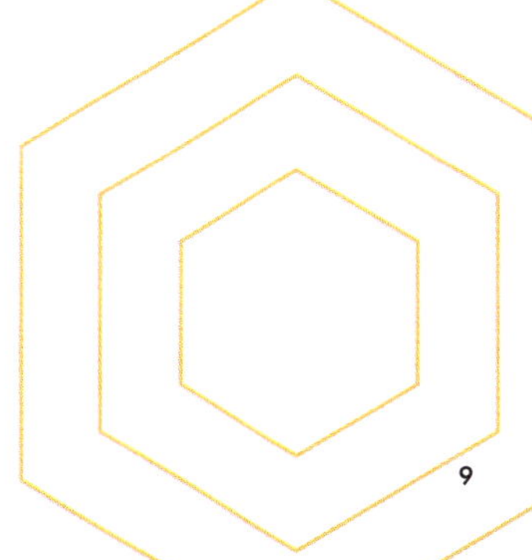

DAY 1

All Day, Every Day

**Keep me safe, O God,
for I have come to You
for refuge. I said to the LORD,
"You are my Master!
Every good thing I have
comes from You. . . . LORD,
You alone are my inheritance,
my cup of blessing.
You guard all that is mine."**

PSALM 16:1–2, 5

[Jesus said,] "Look at the lilies of the field and how they grow. They don't work or make their clothing, yet Solomon in all his glory was not dressed as beautifully as they are. And if God cares so wonderfully for wildflowers that are here today and thrown into the fire tomorrow, He will certainly care for you. . . .

"So don't worry about these things, saying, 'What will we eat? What will we drink? What will we wear?' These things dominate the thoughts of unbelievers, but your heavenly Father already knows all your needs. Seek the Kingdom of God above all else, and live righteously, and He will give you everything you need" (Matthew 6:28–33).

The faithful love of the LORD never ends! . . . Great is His faithfulness; His mercies begin afresh each morning. I say to myself, "The LORD is my inheritance; therefore, I will hope in Him!" (Lamentations 3:22–24)

Teach those who are rich in this world not to be proud and not to trust in their money, which is so unreliable. Their trust should be in God, who richly gives us all we need for our enjoyment (I Timothy 6:17).

Keep me safe, O God, for I have come to You for refuge. I said to the LORD, "You are my Master! Every good thing I have comes from You. . . . LORD, You alone are my inheritance, my cup of blessing. You guard all that is mine." (Psalm 16:1–2, 5)

A NOTE FROM CANDACE

ALL DAY, EVERY DAY

Of all the chapters in the Bible, Matthew 6 could most accurately be called the "Don't Worry" chapter. One thing I love about it is that Jesus speaks to us directly, assuring us, "I've got you. I know your needs. I see you, every minute of every day." But leaning in to those reassurances doesn't always come easily, does it? We have all experienced times when the worries of this life popped up and stopped us from doing all that we were capable of.

Two things strike me about the message of Matthew 6. First is *how dependent we all are*. It's not just the birds and the wildflowers. It's us too! Although my three kids are grown now (I feel you, fellow empty nesters!), I can remember the first months of their lives. They needed their dad and me, as sleep-deprived as we were, to figure out what their cries meant and respond accordingly—diaper changes, more milk, or another nap. Infants rely on Mommy and Daddy, and they thrive and grow.

Could it be that relying on our Father in heaven produces the same results for us? Is our dependence on Him one of the ways He ensures that we thrive? It sure seems like it by this passage!

The second thing I notice in Matthew 6 is that *there's real freedom in not having to worry about our daily needs*. As verse 32 says, that's a huge difference between those who know God and those who don't. For those who don't know Him, their thoughts are dominated by anxiety. But being sure that you can trust the One who is looking out for you means you can breathe easier. You can sleep better and live bolder because you're not being crushed by worry.

I have a living example of this in my household with my fur beast, Boris. He's an absolutely enormous dog. Yet he can't pour even a tiny bit of water into his own dish. He relies on his humans to make sure his needs are met. Does that bother him? No! Boris sleeps like a champ (on my bed, ugh) and wakes up every morning, eager to enjoy another day. He can do that because he knows he's covered. We are looking out for him.

If you think about it, we're all able to live fully in *any* relationship when we can count on the One who is caring for us. God shows up for us all day, every day. He can't *not* do that! Being steadfast and faithful and loving is what He does and who He is.

Trust Him. "He will most certainly care for you."

THINK ON IT

When was the last time you were rolling along and some worry popped up and crowded out your joy? What was that worry, and what did you do with it?

Which two or three worries have been most frequently on your mind?

Lamentations 3:23 tells us, "His mercies begin afresh each morning." Apply this to your everyday worries. What does this mean for you? What difference does it make to have new mercies, fresh mercies, from heaven to rely on when you wake up each day?

THINK ON IT

Even if you were never taught the Lord's Prayer growing up, you've probably heard it quoted during an anxious scene in a movie or on TV. Jesus' best-known prayer includes this request: "Give us this day our daily bread" (Matthew 6:11 KJV). What was His wisdom in this? Why do you think He guided us to ask our Father in heaven for only the food we need today?

Exodus 16:35 says the Lord provided for His people each day for forty years as they traveled through the wilderness to the Promised Land. Nehemiah 9 additionally testifies, "In Your great mercy You did not abandon them to die in the wilderness. The pillar of cloud still led them forward by day, and the pillar of fire showed them the way through the night. You sent Your good Spirit to instruct them, and You did not stop giving them manna [food] from heaven or water for their thirst. For forty years You sustained them in the wilderness, and they lacked nothing. Their clothes did not wear out, and their feet did not swell!" (verses 19–21). If the Lord would take such unfailing care of a million or so people for decades, what does that mean for His intent and ability to take care of you?

ACT ON IT

Besides knowing the One you rely on, rejoicing in God's provision for this day is a great way to leave its worries behind. You can "replace" your worries with praises. Let's do that right now.

In the left-hand column on the chart below, list your concerns of the next twenty-four hours. Then take a minute to ask God how to turn these worries into rejoicing. Sit in the stillness and let Him whisper His ideas to you. As He does, write down those praises in the right-hand column and keep adding to the list as more of them come to mind. (For example, maybe you're worried about passing a certification exam this afternoon. You can replace this worry with a praise by thanking God for giving you the intelligence and the opportunity to go after a career goal.)

MY CONCERNS	MY PRAISES

This is the day the LORD has made.
We will rejoice and be glad in it.

PSALM 118:24

Pop on over for a video from me (Candace) on today's topic!

The Nightwatch

I will bless the LORD
who guides me;
even at night my heart
instructs me.
I know the LORD
is always with me.
I will not be shaken,
for He is right beside me.

PSALM 16:7–8

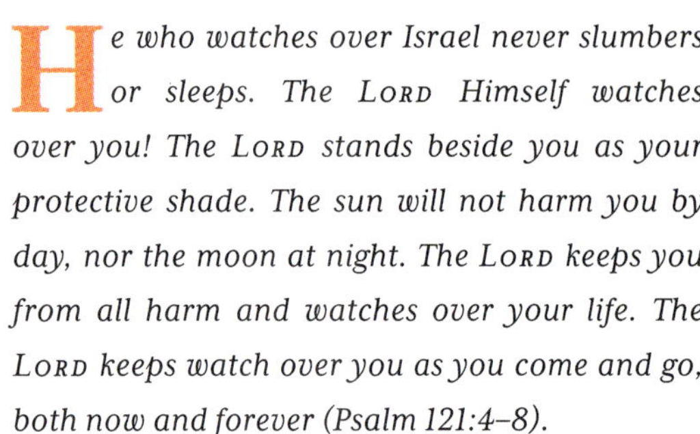

He who watches over Israel never slumbers or sleeps. The LORD Himself watches over you! The LORD stands beside you as your protective shade. The sun will not harm you by day, nor the moon at night. The LORD keeps you from all harm and watches over your life. The LORD keeps watch over you as you come and go, both now and forever (Psalm 121:4–8).

The LORD is my shepherd; I have all that I need. He lets me rest in green meadows; He leads me beside peaceful streams. He renews my strength (Psalm 23:1–3).

In peace I will lie down and sleep, for You alone, O LORD, will keep me safe (Psalm 4:8).

I will bless the LORD who guides me; even at night my heart instructs me. I know the LORD is always with me. I will not be shaken, for He is right beside me (Psalm 16:7–8).

[Jesus told His disciples,] "I will not abandon you as orphans. . . . What I am telling you is from the Father who sent Me. I am telling you these things now while I am still with you. But when the Father sends the Advocate as My representative—that is, the Holy Spirit—He will teach you everything and will remind you of everything I have told you" (John 14:18, 24–26).

"Be sure of this: I am with you always, even to the end of the age" (Matthew 28:20).

A NOTE FROM CANDACE

THE NIGHTWATCH

Ask any toddler mom. Few things are more exhausting than having to keep a constant eye out to make sure that little one stays safe. (PS: Should you ever need an antidote to insomnia, chase a little ball of energy from morning to night. You'll be ready for bedtime before you know it!)

There's also the bone-wearying vigilance of watching over someone you love who is seriously ill or who can no longer take care of themselves.

Unsettling events make me especially thankful for the comfort of Psalm 121:4, that our God never dozes. Never falls asleep at the wheel. Never clocks out or goes on vacation. He handles the nightwatch—and He's on duty all day too.

What a difference that makes! Can you imagine how vigilant we would have to be if we never knew when He was awake? How alone we would feel?

When the birth of Jesus was foretold by Isaiah the prophet and confirmed to Joseph by the angel in Matthew 1, the Lord declared that His name should be Immanuel, which means "God is with us." Of all Jesus' names or titles in Scripture, this one probably means the most to me personally. God the Father sent His Son! To earth! To be with us!

Once Jesus had completed His earthly mission of dying as a substitute for our sins and defeating death by being resurrected from the grave, He sent the Holy Spirit to live permanently inside every believer. This divinely orchestrated plan communicates loud and clear that heaven has always had us in mind. To this day, God is with us, watching over us. We are never alone.

I think about that a lot, particularly when I'm battling worry. Worry is based in fear, and fear typically arises from feelings of helplessness, abandonment, or loneliness. But Somebody who loves us is on the lookout, always by our side, never sleeping so that we *can* sleep.

When God tells His warriors again and again in the Bible, "Do not fear" or "Do not be afraid," He's not kidding! We can rest because God remains with us. We can have peace in scary circumstances, not because there is nothing to fear but because God is with us. Right now. At this moment that you're reading these words.

Do you hear Him? "Do not be afraid. I am with you, both now and forever."

THINK ON IT

What's the longest you've ever had to be "on watch"? What was the situation?

How long were you able to remain that way before the weariness hit?
What other effects did the constant vigilance have on you?

THINK ON IT

Theologian Helmut Thielicke said this about Jesus coming to earth: "Jesus Christ did not remain at base headquarters in heaven, receiving reports of the world's suffering from below and shouting a few encouraging words to us from a safe distance. No, He left the headquarters and came down to us in the front-line trenches, right down to where we live." Besides His great love for us, why would Jesus do this? What are some additional reasons?*

John 1:14 says, "The Word became human and made His home among us. He was full of unfailing love and faithfulness. And we have seen His glory, the glory of the Father's one and only Son." What difference does it make for all people that God the Father wanted the world to see and know Jesus in the flesh? What difference does it make for you?

* Helmut Thielicke, *Christ and the Meaning of Life: A Book of Sermons and Meditations* (Cambridge, United Kingdom: Lutterworth Press, 2016).

ACT ON IT

In Isaiah 7:14, the prophet foretold the coming of Immanuel. Isaiah 9:6 lists several other names for Jesus, the coming Messiah: "He will be called: Wonderful Counselor, Mighty God, Everlasting Father, Prince of Peace."

The various names or titles for Christ throughout Scripture (nearly two hundred in all) aren't meant to confuse, and they definitely don't contradict each other. They continually reveal further aspects of Jesus's character, works, and many roles.

Below are the four names of Christ from Isaiah 9:6—each of them a different representation of "God is with us." Beside each one, journal about what this name means to you personally and a current or recent situation in your life where you saw this aspect of Jesus.

Wonderful Counselor

Mighty God

Everlasting Father

Prince of Peace

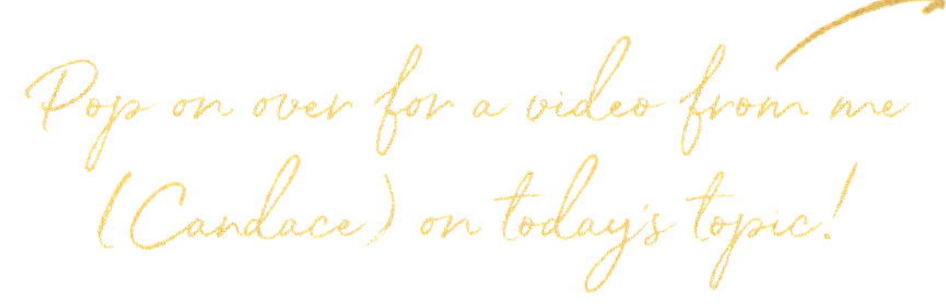

DAY 3

Failure Isn't Fatal

We know that God causes everything to work together for the good of those who love God and are called according to His purpose for them.

ROMANS 8:28

Tune your ears to wisdom, and concentrate on understanding. Cry out for insight, and ask for understanding. Search for them as you would for silver; seek them like hidden treasures. Then you will understand what it means to fear the LORD, and you will gain knowledge of God (Proverbs 2:2–5).

[Jesus said,] "God blesses those who are poor and realize their need for Him, for the Kingdom of Heaven is theirs. God blesses those who mourn, for they will be comforted. God blesses those who are humble, for they will inherit the whole earth" (Matthew 5:3–5).

We know that God causes everything to work together for the good of those who love God and are called according to His purpose for them (Romans 8:28).

If you reject discipline, you only harm yourself; but if you listen to correction, you grow in understanding. Fear of the LORD teaches wisdom; humility precedes honor (Proverbs 15:32–33).

A NOTE FROM CANDACE

FAILURE ISN'T FATAL

In my "warrior learning curve," I'm discovering that it's okay to fail.

That's been really big for me. Throughout my life, my worries haven't revolved around the crises that could happen as much as around doubt. The things I worry about most tend to be performance-driven: Am I good enough? Can I do this? Will I be able to achieve what I'm striving for?

I hate to think how much time and energy I've lost over the years wondering, *What if I can't? What if I don't?* At least I'm seeing change for the better as my faith grows.

What's changed for me isn't caring any less about my goals. I'm simply realizing that the learning is sometimes the lesson. There's a particular kind of triumph in trying that we can't acheive if we never take a risk.

Leadership expert John Maxwell released a book several years ago titled *Failing Forward*. That's a good way to describe how my perspective is changing. For every failure of ours, God's grace prevails so that we can still move forward. He extends grace to us, and we can then give grace to ourselves, confident that He works all things together for those who love Him.

Believe me, I don't always accomplish what I intend. I get rejected for roles; not every business venture works out; I've disappointed myself as a parent and a wife and a performer. But did I learn? Was I pursuing God's purposes? Am I growing from it? If I can say yes, then it wasn't a failure. God was with me in those moments. And though they didn't turn out the way I hoped, the fact that I said yes and tried still qualifies me as a warrior.

Melinda Gates reframes failure in a similar way. In a 2017 interview with *Good Housekeeping*, she remarked: "We had failures all the time at Microsoft, but the way I see it, failures are things you learn from. . . . That's what I love about sports: For young girls, you want to keep their confidence up, have them play a team sport, because guess what? You step out of bounds, and the game goes on three seconds later."*

What a great perspective! Failure is something temporary that teaches and trains us; it's not who we are, and it should never be treated as a defining moment that we have to spend our lives compensating for.

Take what you can from those experiences, apply the lessons to your next venture, and then reenter the game. Nothing can hold back a warrior who is willing to live and learn.

* Melinda Gates, "Melinda Gates Shares Her 10 Tips for Making the World a Better Place," *Good Housekeeping*, August 14, 2017, https://www.goodhousekeeping.com/life/inpirational-stories/a45546/awesome-women-awards-melinda-gates/.

THINK ON IT

When was the last time you experienced what you or others might consider a failure?

How did you view it at the time?

THINK ON IT

As time has passed, have you begun to view it differently? In what ways? What has changed?

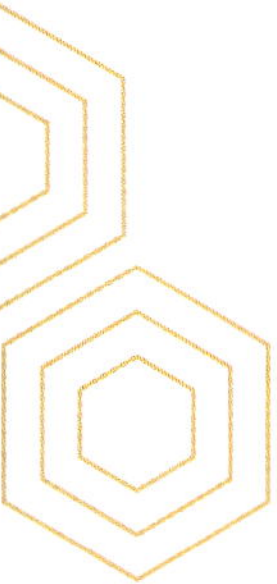

Romans 8:28 reminds us that God brings good out of both our successes and our failures when we are pursuing His purposes. What's the greatest good you've seen Him produce out of a failure or the most valuable lesson you've learned?

ACT ON IT

Because our words have power, here's a chance for you to reframe this entire concept. Below, fill in the numbered list on the left with ten phrases or terms that you or the people you know commonly use to refer to failure.

In the numbered list on the right, start to build a new vocabulary—one that reflects what God can do and what you're learning as you get to know Him and His perspective. (Example: "Falling down" could be reclassified as "Falling forward.") With time and practice, you'll notice the more positive wording seeping into your attitude and your outlook. This is one way that God transforms us.

FAILURE	REFRAMED
1	1
2	2
3	3
4	4
5	5
6	6
7	7

Pop on over for a video from me (Candace) on today's topic!

DAY 4

Watch Where You Look

Do your best to present yourself to God as one approved, a worker who has no need to be ashamed, rightly handling the word of truth.

II TIMOTHY 2:15 ESV

My eyes are always on the LORD, for He rescues me from the traps of my enemies (Psalm 25:15).

Sensible people keep their eyes glued on wisdom, but a fool's eyes wander to the ends of the earth (Proverbs 17:24).

Pray in the Spirit at all times and on every occasion. Stay alert and be persistent in your prayers for all believers everywhere (Ephesians 6:18).

A prudent person foresees danger and takes precautions. The simpleton goes blindly on and suffers the consequences (Proverbs 27:12).

It was by faith that Moses left the land of Egypt, not fearing the king's anger. He kept right on going because he kept his eyes on the one who is invisible (Hebrews 11:27).

Do your best to present yourself to God as one approved, a worker who has no need to be ashamed, rightly handling the word of truth (II Timothy 2:15 ESV).

A NOTE FROM CANDACE

WATCH WHERE YOU LOOK

When the army of ancient Israel was about to go to battle against the Midianites, God told their leader, Gideon: "You have too many warriors with you. If I let all of you fight the Midianites, the Israelites will boast to Me that they saved themselves by their own strength." So God said to Gideon, "Whoever is timid or afraid may leave this mountain and go home" (Judges 7:2–3). Of the thirty-two thousand that Gideon started with, twenty-two thousand soldiers exited at that point.

The ten thousand who remained were still too many. So the Lord told Gideon to take those men to a nearby stream and test them. Those who drank like a dog, head down and lapping up the water with their tongues, were sent home. Those who cupped the water in their hands and then put it to their mouths made the final cut. Gideon was left with three hundred warriors. Three hundred men who were naturally watching for the enemy and were ready to win the battle (verses 4–9).

Where is *your* focus right now? Self-sabotaging thoughts or emotions can show up anytime, anywhere, just as surely as an enemy can. Those saboteurs inside us can distract us until we're consumed with anxiety or feeling too defeated to fight. So we warriors have to watch where we're looking.

Today, if you sense something sinister creeping up behind you—upsetting your stomach, tightening your muscles, making it difficult for you to concentrate, causing you to growl at the people you love—check yourself. Are you

- looking inward, self-absorbed, with an eye out for number one?
- looking backward with a heart that won't forgive?
- looking down in defeat?
- looking around in fear, wondering where the next attack will come from?
- looking back and forth in comparison (which creates its own form of anxiety and stress)?

The disciplines of spending time in prayer and in God's Word are what help me direct—and redirect—my mind, my eyes, and my heart on a daily basis. They're how I train to avoid an ambush. Having accountability with prayer partners or mentors is also a huge plus.

The way to fight off saboteurs of any kind is to make yourself a difficult target. Discourage them by looking up with hope! Look around you with faith! Look ahead with great confidence! Most importantly, look to your Leader and His truth. You're in the Lord's army, and *He* gives the victory!

THINK ON IT

How do you know when your focus starts to stray?
What are your telltale signs of self-sabotage?

In a typical week, do you think you are mostly expectant and mindful, or unaware and distracted? Explain your answer and where that tendency comes from.

THINK ON IT

Proverbs 27:12 says, "A prudent person foresees danger and takes precautions. The simpleton goes blindly on and suffers the consequences." When was the last time you saw danger ahead and ignored it? What were the consequences?

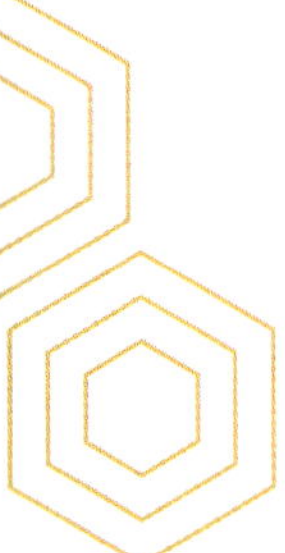

What would watchfulness look like for you? (A lot of people find that the ACTS approach to prayer each day centers their attention in the right place: A—adoration, or worshiping God; C—confession of sins; T—thanksgiving; S—supplication, which means bringing requests to the Lord.)

How can you apply the wisdom on the Scripture page to maintain the kind of spiritual focus that will bring you victory over negativity?

ACT ON IT

Over the next week, keep track of where your attention centers the most each day, using the chart below. Consider it an "eye chart" of sorts. You can assign a percentage or draw emojis, arrows, or some other type of symbol in the middle column for a record of where you've focused your eyes that day and include a brief *why* on the right for reference. What caused you to look in that direction?

At the end of the week, assess yourself. As you prayerfully review the chart, ask God to give you some ideas for improvement. Write those in the space below the chart.

	THE DIRECTION I LOOKED	WHY
Monday		
Tuesday		
Wednesday		
Thursday		
Friday		
Saturday		
Sunday		

Ideas for Improving My "Eyesight" ______________________________

____

____

Pop on over for a video from me (Candace) on today's topic!

DAY 5

Does It Help?

Commit everything you do to the LORD. Trust Him, and He will help you.

PSALM 37:5

Jesus said,] "I tell you not to worry about everyday life—whether you have enough food and drink, or enough clothes to wear. . . . Look at the birds. They don't plant or harvest or store food in barns, for your heavenly Father feeds them. And aren't you far more valuable to Him than they are? Can all your worries add a single moment to your life?" (Matthew 6:25–27)

Commit everything you do to the LORD. Trust Him, and He will help you (Psalm 37:5).

I love God's law with all my heart. But there is another power within me that is at war with my mind. . . . Who will free me from this life that is dominated by sin and death? Thank God! The answer is in Jesus Christ our Lord (Romans 7:22–25).

Be strong in the Lord and in His mighty power. Put on all of God's armor so that you will be able to stand firm against all strategies of the devil (Ephesians 6:10–11).

Nothing can ever separate us from God's love. Neither death nor life, neither angels nor demons, neither our fears for today nor our worries about tomorrow—not even the powers of hell can separate us from . . . the love of God that is revealed in Christ Jesus our Lord (Romans 8:38–39).

There is no condemnation for those who belong to Christ Jesus. And because you belong to Him, the power of the life-giving Spirit has freed you from the power of sin that leads to death (Romans 8:1–2).

A NOTE FROM CANDACE

DOES IT HELP?

In Matthew 6:27, Jesus makes a really good point: Does all your worrying help? Does it enhance your life in any way?

We all know the answer: *Nope. Being anxious does NOT help.* Does that stop us from worrying? Um, not often enough.

Gulp.

This is the kind of stuff that sometimes drives me crazy about myself! I'm not a big worrier by nature, but when I do get in worry mode, I can hang with the best of 'em. To recognize that I'm only hurting myself but then keep worrying anyway . . . well, that's about as frustrating as it gets!

I know I'm not the only one who has ever felt this way. The apostle Paul, who wrote much of the New Testament, wrestled with the same sort of struggle. I'm so thankful for his transparency in his letter to fellow Christians in ancient Rome: "I don't really understand myself, for I want to do what is right, but I don't do it. Instead, I do what I hate" (Romans 7:15).

Why do we do this to ourselves? Spiritually speaking, it's because we're opting to live by the sin nature each of us was born with rather than by the Spirit, the Holy Spirit who lives inside every follower of Christ. He is the one who divinely "in-powers" believers with wisdom, faith, and strength to follow God and choose His ways.

Humanly speaking, I suppose we resort to worry because it makes us feel like we're doing something. But worrying is not doing. A worrier is someone who stays in her thoughts, turning the problem over and over again like a lump of overworked dough. In contrast, a warrior turns worry into action. She puts faith to work, consistently exercising her spiritual muscles by

- spending consistent time in God's Word, which serves as a guide for her steps and a light for her path;
- seeking the Lord in prayer for His will in her decisions;
- giving *all* her worries and cares to Him;
- confessing her sins and trusting in God's forgiveness so that nothing stands between them;
- armoring up against the enemy and his attacks.

If you aren't so sure about how to take that first step of action toward being a spiritual warrior, try praying the honest words of a father to Jesus in Mark 9:24: "I do believe, but help me overcome my unbelief!"

He will. Just ask.

THINK ON IT

What's your typical response to worry? Why is this your go-to?

How does getting stuck in the loop of worry feel to you?
What would you compare it to?

THINK ON IT

Ephesians 6:13 commands us to "put on every piece of God's armor" as we fight, for it helps us stand firm and resist the enemy. Verses 14–18 specify that once we have put on the helmet of salvation and have the sword of the Spirit (the Word of God) in hand, we should "hold up the shield of faith to stop the fiery arrows of the devil." We must also put on "the belt of truth and the body armor of God's righteousness" and the shoes of peace that come from the good news of the gospel. Finally, we're told to "pray in the Spirit at all times and on every occasion."

In what ways are you already armored up? What armor do you need to put on?

What are three to five immediate steps you can take to quit worrying and start exercising your faith?

ACT ON IT

My definition of taking action includes trusting that my heavenly Father walks with me and cherishes me and will never leave me, just as He says in His Word. To imagine God walking with me through my day can be a real trust builder. I actually picture Him beside me, talking with me and looking at me with love!

At least three times this week, plan to bring that visual to life during your lunch break or at either end of your day by going on an actual walk with Him. Talk to Jesus out loud, just like you would your best friend. Envision the Lord walking next to you, holding your hand like a caring friend. And just as you would in any conversation, allow some moments of silence after you've poured out your heart so that His Spirit can guide you, speak to you, comfort you, encourage you.

After each walk, journal here about the topics you shared and what God imparted to you as you walked with Him.

Walk #1 ________________________

Walk #2 ________________________

Walk #3 ________________________

Give all your worries and cares to God, for He cares about you.

I PETER 5:7

Silence!

In that coming day no weapon turned against you will succeed. You will silence every voice raised up to accuse you. These benefits are enjoyed by the servants of the LORD; their vindication will come from Me. I, the LORD, have spoken!

ISAIAH 54:17

The Philistines now mustered their army for battle. . . . Saul countered by gathering his Israelite troops near the valley of Elah. So the Philistines and Israelites faced each other on opposite hills, with the valley between them. Then Goliath, a Philistine champion from Gath, came out of the Philistine ranks to face the forces of Israel.

He was over nine feet tall! He wore a bronze helmet, and his bronze coat of mail weighed 125 pounds. He also wore bronze leg armor, and he carried a bronze javelin on his shoulder. The shaft of his spear was as heavy and thick as a weaver's beam, tipped with an iron spearhead that weighed 15 pounds. His armor bearer walked ahead of him carrying a shield.

Goliath stood and shouted a taunt across to the Israelites. "Why are you all coming out to fight?" he called. "I am the Philistine champion, but you are only the servants of Saul. Choose one man to come down here and fight me! If he kills me, then we will be your slaves. But if I kill him, you will be our slaves! I defy the armies of Israel today! Send me a man who will fight me!" (I Samuel 17:1–10)

Watch out for your great enemy, the devil. He prowls around like a roaring lion, looking for someone to devour. Stand firm against him, and be strong in your faith (I Peter 5:8–9).

In that coming day no weapon turned against you will succeed. You will silence every voice raised up to accuse you. These benefits are enjoyed by the servants of the Lord*; their vindication will come from Me. I, the Lord, have spoken! (Isaiah 54:17)*

You are my King and my God. You command victories for Israel. Only by Your power can we push back our enemies; only in Your name can we trample our foes. I do not trust in my bow; I do not count on my sword to save me. You are the one who gives us victory over our enemies; You disgrace those who hate us. O God, we give glory to You all day long and constantly praise Your name (Psalm 44:4–8).

A NOTE FROM CANDACE

SILENCE!

The giant Goliath, of David and Goliath fame, didn't just stand head and shoulders above everybody else on the battlefield. We're told that each time he came out of his tent to threaten the army of Israel, he wore a load of armor, including a heavy bronze helmet, and brought a full stash of weapons—a spear, a javelin, and a sword—in addition to having a shield.

Isn't that interesting? I mean, if you were that tall, looming over every opponent, would you really need a suit of armor? Why carry a bunch of weapons? It makes me think Goliath was hiding something—some insecurity, some weakness. Or that he was secretly afraid. Behind all the fist-pumping and chest-beating was perhaps the false bravado of an opponent who knew he wasn't so mighty after all.

This is true of a lot of bullies, isn't it? They have a loud bark . . . as long as no one stands up to them. It wasn't until David came along that someone from Israel was strong enough in their faith to stand up to Goliath and actually challenge him.

In a very real sense, temptation is one of life's most persistent bullies. If it's not attempting a sneak attack ("C'mon, just one brownie. One brownie won't hurt you"), it's trying to intimidate us into submission with threatening words. Yet I've found that most of the time, if I resist right away and keep resisting, the shouting stops and the temptation eventually retreats.

That's what happened in the wilderness when Satan tried to tempt Jesus to sin. Satan came at Jesus with three increasingly powerful "lusts" in succession, and each time Jesus shut down the tempter with words from Scripture. After Satan's third failed attempt, he gave up and went away, leaving Jesus alone.

If you think about it, a lion's roar—as scary as it is—is just a wall of sound. The roar itself can't hurt you. God has equipped us to repel attacks in many ways that we talk about in this devotional guide, and silencing the tempter's roar is one of our best counterefforts.

So the next time temptation comes out of its tent, seeking to accuse you, wound you, shame you, insult you, or freeze you with shouts or lies, don't sit there and fret about it. Talk over it! Quote Bible verses back at it. it. Play praise music in its face. Put temptation's half-truths and outright lies to the test, asking the Holy Spirit and your friends, "Please remind me of what *is* true." And keep resisting with a hard *no*!

God promises that, with His help, we can turn away our adversary. Isn't that great news? I'm all for shutting him down and sending him on his way! Are you with me?

THINK ON IT

As he did when tempting Jesus, Satan claims he can satisfy our cravings, our egos, our desire for wealth or fame if only we will worship him (Matthew 4:1–11). Which of these areas is the hardest for you to resist?

Think of the last time you were tempted in a big way and successfully resisted. What was the temptation? How long did it last?

THINK ON IT

What tactics did you use to overcome it? How soon did the temptation go away once you said no?

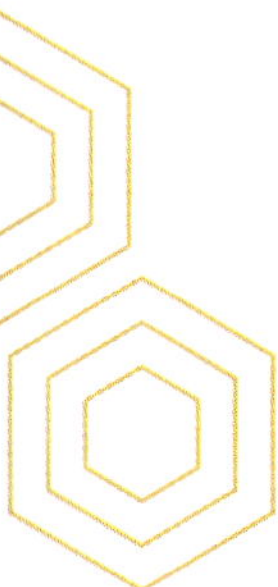

How prepared were you? Did you expect the temptation?
What kinds of defenses did you already have in place?

Jesus's public ministry began right after He turned away the devil. Temptations and trials often precede great productivity for God's kingdom. What important work do you think God has ahead for you if you will resist the enemy and stay devoted to the Lord?

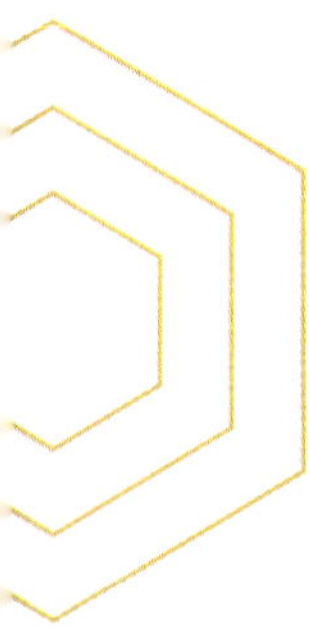

ACT ON IT

So much of what we worry about revolves around the threat of temptation: "What if this happens?" or "What if I'm faced with that?" But you are not powerless, dear warrior! Take some time in the space below to list some of the "what-ifs" that tend to talk at you the most—the temptations that you face regularly. But instead of writing what could go wrong, answer those concerns with what could go right and how God has specifically equipped you to stand your ground.

WHAT IFS	BEST POSSIBLE OUTCOME

Pop on over for a video from me (Candace) on today's topic!

DAY 7

Not My Solution!

**Do the will of God
with all your heart.
Work with enthusiasm,
as though you were working for
the Lord rather than for people.
Remember that the Lord
will reward each one of us
for the good we do.**

EPHESIANS 6:6–8

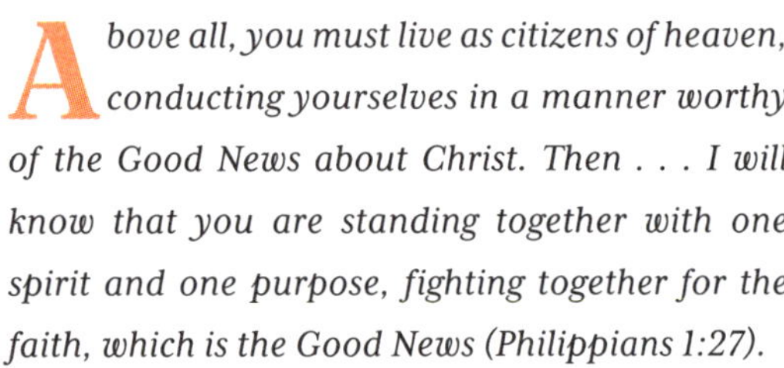

Above all, you must live as citizens of heaven, conducting yourselves in a manner worthy of the Good News about Christ. Then . . . I will know that you are standing together with one spirit and one purpose, fighting together for the faith, which is the Good News (Philippians 1:27).

Live a life filled with love, following the example of Christ. He loved us and offered Himself as a sacrifice for us, a pleasing aroma to God (Ephesians 5:2).

Love your enemies! Do good to those who hate you. Bless those who curse you. Pray for those who hurt you. . . . Give to anyone who asks; and when things are taken away from you, don't try to get them back. Do to others as you would like them to do to you (Luke 6:27–28, 30–31).

Do the will of God with all your heart. Work with enthusiasm, as though you were working for the Lord rather than for people. Remember that the Lord will reward each one of us for the good we do (Ephesians 6:6–8).

A NOTE FROM CANDACE

NOT MY SOLUTION!

A big part of my faith is knowing God will provide a solution. Many times I've seen Him provide completely for me or someone I've prayed for, handling every detail on our behalf. Other times, God has invited me to partner with Him to be part of the solution.

I'm usually all about that partnering thing. I've particularly loved it when God has called Val and me to serve Him with our kids. Teaming up as a family for a missions trip overseas or to help out at local food pantries and homeless shelters in our area has allowed us to meet some truly beautiful souls who have enriched our faith.

There are times, though, where being on God's team tests me—hard. Times when His solution is not my solution. Times when I'd rather He choose someone else.

In Exodus 3–4, God called Moses to join Him in leading the Israelites out of slavery in Egypt. Moses' responses sounded like mine do sometimes: "I am not equipped." . . . "Who am I to do that?" . . . "What will I say?" Despite His servant's hesitations and insecurities, God used Moses to do a mighty work.

Though our individual situations will look different, the decision for every warrior is the same: Will I sign up and be part of God's answer *in the way that He asks*?

It might mean humbling myself and being the first to apologize, the first to forgive, the first to reach out or speak up and take a stand.

It could involve saying no to good options for the sake of having more time for family.

It may require rearranging a weekend schedule or making some room in the budget to be able to help someone in need.

More often than not, being on God's team will involve doing as Jesus did: Turning the other cheek. Praying for our enemies. Putting others ahead of ourselves. Serving to the point of sacrifice.

Whether or not God's solution is what you would choose, serve anyway, warriors—to the best of your ability. Be part of His answer. Whatever He asks, commit yourself fully to the mission. Sometimes He provides for us—and sometimes through us. His method doesn't matter, and neither does the size of the ask. When He calls, answer. That's what family does.

THINK ON IT

Describe a recent situation where people pitched in to help you accomplish a task or a goal. What kind of difference did that make for you?

When God prompts you to join Him in an effort, how often do you let your . . .

- *circumstances*
- *resources (such as time or money)*
- *personality, or*
- *weaknesses*

. . . define what you can do?

Which "category" of excuse do you tend to draw from the most? Why?

THINK ON IT

Philippians 2:14–15 urges, "Do everything without complaining and arguing. . . . Live clean, innocent lives as children of God, shining like bright lights" in the world. To have this gracious spirit isn't just important with others; it's vital in our relationship with God.

In what types of situations does your attitude shine? Which situations tend to provoke your resistance? What do these patterns tell you about yourself? About your relationship with God?

Is God urging you to give up your agenda or independence and serve Him in a specific way—and you just know it? Jot down at least three action steps for changing your attitude or creating space in your life so that you can join in what He is doing.

If nothing comes to mind right now, be on the lookout, because the RSVP is in the mail! Meanwhile, go ahead and jot down three actions steps you should take in order to be ready.

ACT ON IT

What are the words you say or the thoughts you think when God asks you to team up with Him to do something outside the box? For each excuse you have this week, in the bubbles below write down the words you used or the thoughts that came to mind (even if you didn't say them out loud). This will give you a good picture of your typical responses.

Once those are represented, reread each one. As you do, pray that you would have the servant attitude and humble heart of Jesus, and then imagine yourself popping each bubble.

OPTION: If you're a tactile learner, you could express your commitment tangibly. Grab a small box and several slips of paper, along with a marker. On the pieces of paper, write the various excuses you listed here. Then throw them in the box, close the lid, and with a prayer of renewed surrender, either drop those excuses in a recycling bin or burn them in the trash.

Pop on over for a video from me (Candace) on today's topic!

DAY 8

Captivated

Don't be selfish; don't try to impress others. Be humble, thinking of others as better than yourselves. Don't look out only for your own interests, but take an interest in others, too. You must have the same attitude that Christ Jesus had.

PHILIPPIANS 2:3–5

Now there was a wealthy and influential man in Bethlehem named Boaz, who was a relative of Naomi's husband, Elimelech.

One day Ruth the Moabite said to Naomi, "Let me go out into the harvest fields to pick up the stalks of grain left behind by anyone who is kind enough to let me do it."

Naomi replied, "All right, my daughter, go ahead." So Ruth went out to gather grain behind the harvesters. And as it happened, she found herself working in a field that belonged to Boaz, the relative of her father-in-law, Elimelech.

While she was there, Boaz arrived from Bethlehem and greeted the harvesters. "The Lord be with you!" he said.

"The Lord bless you!" the harvesters replied.

Then Boaz asked his foreman, "Who is that young woman over there?" . . .

And the foreman replied, "She is the young woman from Moab who came back with Naomi. She asked me this morning if she could gather grain behind the harvesters. She has been hard at work ever since, except for a few minutes' rest in the shelter."

Boaz went over and said to Ruth, "Listen, my daughter. Stay right here with us when you gather grain; don't go to any other fields. Stay right behind the young women working in my field. See which part of the field they are harvesting, and then follow them. I have warned the young men not to treat you roughly. And when you are thirsty, help yourself to the water they have drawn from the well."

Ruth fell at his feet and thanked him warmly. "What have I done to deserve such kindness?" she asked. "I am only a foreigner."

"Yes, I know," Boaz replied. "But I also know about everything you have done for your mother-in-law since the death of your husband. I have heard how you left your father and mother and your own land to live here among complete strangers. May the Lord, the God of Israel, under whose wings you have come to take refuge, reward you fully for what you have done" (Ruth 2:1–12).

Mordecai sent this reply to Esther: "Don't think for a moment that because you're in the palace you will escape when all other Jews are killed. If you keep quiet at a time like this, deliverance and relief for the Jews will arise from some other place, but you and your relatives will die. Who knows if perhaps you were made queen for just such a time as this?" (Esther 4:13–14)

The Lord said to Samuel [about one of David's brothers], "Don't judge by his appearance or height, for I have rejected him. The Lord doesn't see things the way you see them. People judge by outward appearance, but the Lord looks at the heart" (I Samuel 16:7).

Don't be selfish; don't try to impress others. Be humble, thinking of others as better than yourselves. Don't look out only for your own interests, but take an interest in others, too. You must have the same attitude that Christ Jesus had (Philippians 2:3–5).

A NOTE FROM CANDACE

CAPTIVATED

One of my favorite roles has been Aurora Teagarden, the librarian-turned-crime-solver in Hallmark's mystery series. Based on the amount of attention her outfits always received, I sometimes think people tuned in to see what she was wearing almost as much as what crime she was investigating!

Did I mind? Of course not! Part of the fun of my job is finding out what the wardrobe department has planned for my characters. Besides, anybody who knows me knows that I'm a sucker for a well-put-together ensemble. Nothing builds up a woman's confidence like a great fit and fabric in her best colors!

Sometimes, though, if we're not careful, we can get too hung up on how we look and overlook the stuff inside us that really, really counts. So every once in a while I need to pause and take a little self-inventory: Am I going through my day worrying more about my clothes or my character? Has my mind been on style or wisdom? Am I comparing myself with others and getting sidelined by it?

"We won't be distracted by comparison if we are captivated with purpose," observes author Bob Goff.* That's what I want to be enamored with: God's purpose for me and my family and our world, like Ruth and Esther from the Bible

In the love story that is the book of Ruth, the young widow Ruth cannot marry the man who loves her until he has followed cultural protocols. Still, Boaz assures her: "Don't worry about a thing. . . . I will do what is necessary, for everyone in town knows you are a virtuous woman" (Ruth 3:11).

Whew! Now THAT, ladies, is a compliment!

Then there's the incredible saga of Esther. She became queen of Persia for winning a beauty contest and capturing the king's heart. More importantly, she had such character that when her husband repeatedly asked her, "What do you want, Queen Esther? What is your request? I will give it to you, even if it is half the kingdom!" (Esther 5:3; see Esther 9:12), never once did she make a request for herself. She listened to her mentors and asked for things that not only earned the king's trust but ultimately positioned her to save her people, the Jews, from mass extermination.

I'll never turn down the chance to wear a great outfit, but I care most about what I have going on inside of me, because those are my true colors. They're what people on the outside will eventually see. Do I embody faith, hope, and love? Are peace and kindness on my lips? Do I carry myself with godly grace and compassion?

If we have those pieces of our ensemble right, then we're all set. We can enter a room with confidence, knowing the beauty of Christ is ours.

* Bob Goff, *Live in Grace, Walk in Love: A 365-Day Journey* (Nashville: Thomas Nelson, 2019), p. 221.

THINK ON IT

What is your favorite outfit or article of clothing? How does wearing it make you feel?

How often do you dress to impress others? In what situations?

THINK ON IT

According to Galatians 5:22–23, the Holy Spirit produces these qualities in our lives: "love, joy, peace, patience, kindness, goodness, faithfulness, gentleness, and self-control." Some of these come more naturally to us than others. Which ones do you embody much of the time?

Which ones do you need more of? Choose one or two and begin a habit of praying for growth in that area.

ACT ON IT

For each spiritual quality listed in Galatians 5 (see the question at the start of the last page), assign a "true color" to it. What color does that trait make you think of, and why? Have fun with this. Decorate the page with those colors in any way you want.

As an ongoing reminder, each time you go into your closet to select your wardrobe for the day or an occasion, choose an item or accessory in the color of the attribute you think you'll need most. And as you're getting dressed, pray that God will shine through you.

TRUE COLORS

Love

Goodness

Joy

Faithfulness

Peace

Gentleness

Patience

Self-Control

Kindness

Pop on over for a video from me (Candace) on today's topic!

Making Change

I love You, LORD;
You are my strength.
The LORD is my rock,
my fortress, and my savior;
my God is my rock, in whom
I find protection. He is my shield,
the power that saves me,
and my place of safety.

PSALM 18:1–2

When the builders completed the foundation of the Lord's Temple, the priests put on their robes and took their places to blow their trumpets. And the Levites . . . clashed their cymbals to praise the Lord, just as King David had prescribed. With praise and thanks, they sang this song to the Lord:

"He is so good!

His faithful love for Israel endures forever!"

Then all the people gave a great shout, praising the Lord because the foundation of the Lord's Temple had been laid.

But many of the older priests, Levites, and other leaders who had seen the first Temple wept aloud when they saw the new Temple's foundation. The others, however, were shouting for joy. The joyful shouting and weeping mingled together in a loud noise that could be heard far in the distance (Ezra 3:10–13).

On October 17 of that same year, the Lord *sent another message through the prophet Haggai. "Say this to Zerubabbel, governor of Judah, and to Jeshua . . . the high priest, and to the remnant of God's people there in the land: 'Does anyone remember this house—this Temple—in its former splendor? How, in comparison, does it look to you now? It must seem like nothing at all! But now the* Lord *says: Be strong, [governor]. Be strong . . . high priest. Be strong, all you people still left in the land. And now get to work, for I am with you, says the* Lord *of Heaven's Armies. My Spirit remains among you, just as I promised when you came out of Egypt. So do not be afraid'" (Haggai 2:1–5).*

I love You, Lord*; You are my strength. The* Lord *is my rock, my fortress, and my savior; my God is my rock, in whom I find protection. He is my shield, the power that saves me, and my place of safety (Psalm 18:1–2).*

A NOTE FROM CANDACE

MAKING CHANGE

Change is hard. I get that, for sure.

I remember how tough it was for me to transition from career actress to stay-at-home mom when Val's career kept him on the road. I don't regret the decision—it was definitely the right one for our family. But I sure had to work through a lot of feelings before I could surrender my will. That's why I relate so personally to Israel's leaders in Ezra 3.

The foundation for the new temple in Jerusalem had just been laid, and the priests had gathered all God's people to worship the Lord for bringing them to this milestone. It was a milestone because after seventy years of exile in Babylon, God had freed Israel and brought a remnant of His people back to their capital city. They were rebuilding all that the Babylonians had decimated so long ago, and finally, work on God's house had begun.

Not everyone felt like celebrating.

While the younger generations were excited as could be, Israel's leaders were weeping, wailing even. I think the sense isn't just mourning but, at least for some of them, the tears of a tantrum. They wanted the original temple back.

One of the wonders of the ancient world, Solomon's temple had been magnificent and spacious and beautifully handcrafted with cedar, gold, silver, bronze, iron, stone, and precious jewels. It was so lavish that it took nearly two hundred thousand workers almost eight years to build.

The new temple was shaping up to be very *not that*.

The thing is, we can't afford to get stuck in what was. If we do, we will miss everything God is doing right in front of our eyes. So while it's not necessarily easy to hear God's call to Israel in Haggai 2:4–5, He knows what we need: "Be strong. . . . And now get to work."

For us to be able to do that, His further words to Israel are key: "For I am with you. . . . My Spirit remains among you. . . . Do not be afraid."

Looking back on those ten years at home with the kids, I can see now that God had work for me to do that could only be done in that window of time. My husband and I had one shot at raising Natasha, Lev, and Maks, and my new role was an investment in them and *their* future. The Lord also instilled a fresh belief during that season that I try to cling to anytime I'm struggling with change: I always have a future if God is my Architect and Foundation.

THINK ON IT

What event or events are forcing you into a season of change?

Which generation's response in Ezra 3 do you relate to? Why? What's behind your response?

What are the toughest aspects of change for you? What are the upsides you've experienced?

THINK ON IT

Comparing our lives to a race, Paul wrote,
"I have not achieved it, but I focus on this one thing: Forgetting the past and looking forward to what lies ahead, I press on to reach the end of the race and receive the heavenly prize for which God, through Christ Jesus, is calling us" (Philippians 3:13–14).
Laying to rest what has been can open us up to what could be and, even more importantly, to what will be.
What are some healthy ways you can bring closure to the past season?
What do you think finishing that race well will do for you?

Reread God's charge to the people in Haggai 2 at the beginning of this entry. As you seek to rebuild in your season of change—maybe due to an empty nest, life after a breakup or a death, or digging out of the rubble of job loss or illness—which statements stand out to you? How can you begin anticipating the future with more hope and with less worry or complaint?

ACT ON IT

In Haggai 2:5, God was reminding the Israelites, "I made a covenant with you hundreds of years ago, back in Egypt, that I'd see you through to this day, and I've kept My word." He could say the same to you and me as His people today. So as sisters in the Lord, let's make a pact that every time we remember the past, we will remember God's presence with us too.

In the Old Testament (such as Joshua 4), the people of God often placed memorial stones to commemorate His care and miraculous provision. Anyone who passed that way after them would see the stones and know that the Lord had been powerfully present for His people in that place. It would be a permanent reminder for them, too, that He was their true Foundation.

Do that here. As a symbolic altar of worship to God or to represent a new foundation being built, designate each memorial stone with some sort of picture or wording that will help you remember God's presence during the changing seasons of your life. Also consider using marked stones in your landscaping or home decor to bring this exercise to life.

REMEMBER HIS PRESENCE

You are members of God's family. Together, we are His house, built on the foundation of the apostles and the prophets. And the cornerstone is Christ Jesus Himself. We are carefully joined together in Him, becoming a holy temple for the Lord.

EPHESIANS 2:19–21

Pop on over for a video from me (Candace) on today's topic!

Screen Time

Do you think the Scriptures have no meaning? They say that God is passionate that the spirit He has placed within us should be faithful to Him. And He gives grace generously.... So humble yourselves before God. ...Come close to God, and God will come close to you.

JAMES 4:5–8

After telling everyone good-bye, [Jesus] went up into the hills by Himself to pray (Mark 6:46).

Jesus often withdrew to the wilderness for prayer (Luke 5:16).

Do you think the Scriptures have no meaning? They say that God is passionate that the spirit He has placed within us should be faithful to Him. And He gives grace generously. . . . So humble yourselves before God. . . . Come close to God, and God will come close to you (James 4:5–8).

Open my eyes to see the wonderful truths in Your instructions. . . . Turn my eyes from worthless things, and give me life through Your word. . . . Renew my life with Your goodness (Psalm 119:18, 37, 40).

Joyful are people of integrity, who follow the instructions of the Lord. Joyful are those who obey His laws and search for Him with all their hearts. . . . You have charged us to keep Your commandments carefully. Oh, that my actions would consistently reflect Your decrees! Then I will not be ashamed when I compare my life with Your commands. As I learn Your righteous regulations, I will thank You by living as I should! (Psalm 119:1–2, 4–7)

A NOTE FROM CANDACE

SCREEN TIME

Whether you're eighteen or eighty, you likely have at least one "screen" in your life: a television, a computer, a cell phone, a tablet. . . . Our screens can be a great way to keep us connected with the world and the ones we care about. But what about when screen time takes over, distracting us from real life? Or when it actually *adds* to our isolation or worries, as researchers have concluded it often does?

This is one area where my husband and I couldn't be more different. It seems like anytime I get a spare minute in my day, I'm either checking my phone or thinking about what my next social media post might be. Val? He once traded in his smartphone for a flip phone because he felt it was getting too much of his attention! Being Mr. Disciplined, he further decided to answer emails only at set times versus opening them all day long.

He had—and still has—a very grounded perspective: "Why shouldn't my family, my friends, my work have priority? Why should some stranger be able to distract me from making dinner for my wife or golfing with my buddies, simply by pushing a few buttons?"

Due in part to his constant example in this area, I challenged myself to take a break from social media during Christmas week a few years ago. I felt it would be a very practical way to create some space for being present and intentional with my family and friends. This little experiment proved to be such a Godsend that I've made it one of my annual holiday traditions.

More power to you if you're one of those iron-willed women who can turn off the TV or set down your phone anytime you decide to! For the rest of us, we have to *choose* to exit our favorite screen every once in a while. No need to wait until next Christmas either. For starters, why not shoot for the next holi*day* on the calendar? Or one weekend this month?

The first few times you take a screen vacation, you'll probably feel some FOMO (fear of missing out). Simply remind yourself, "Hey, I'm choosing this, and I'm going to make the most of it!" I think you'll discover that what you were really missing out on was a little peace and quiet, and the joy of making memories with your loved ones.

THINK ON IT

How much time do you think you spend on your screen of choice in an average day? What would be your goal, allowing you to feel like you have a good balance between screen time and "life time"?

Have you ever given up screen time on purpose? How much of a challenge was it for you? If you haven't tried this, what do you expect to be your biggest temptation?

THINK ON IT

Think about the last time you planned a vacation. In what ways is this screen vacation similar? How does it feel different to you?

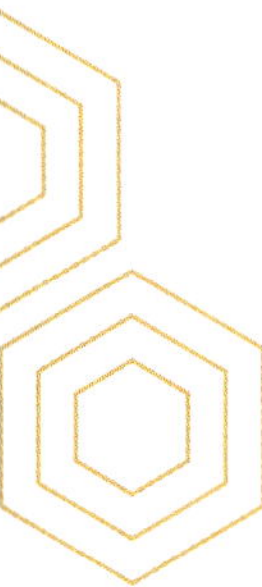

Refer to the two passages from Psalm 119 on the Scripture page. They list several benefits of time with the Lord and in His Word. What's the best thing that a screen holiday could do for you?

ACT ON IT

I want to encourage you: A screen holiday isn't a jail sentence. It's a treasure hunt! So please don't approach it with the attitude of "I'm just going to get through it." Instead, anticipate it. Plan for it. Be intentional about this break so that you can squeeze every last ounce of goodness from it! To help with that, brainstorm your ideal break in advance, starting with the categories and questions below.

WHEN I WILL TAKE MY BREAK

WHAT I'D LIKE TO DO

WHO I'D LIKE TO SEE

WHAT I'M LOOKING FORWARD TO

WHY I'M WILLING TO TRY THIS

Need some ideas for how to spend your time?

- Enjoy nature and some physical exercise.
- Come back to that hobby you set aside months ago.
- Grab coffee with a few friends you haven't seen in a while.
- Do something kind for somebody who needs a pick-me-up.
- Volunteer at a local charity.
- Visit a nearby place of interest you've always wanted to see but never had time for.

And don't forget to spend some quality time with your Father in heaven. He is constantly reaching out to His daughters—nudging our spirits, encouraging our souls, assuring us of why He's so fond of us. Though I've found He often whispers rather than shouts. So leave some space for hearing Him, okay?

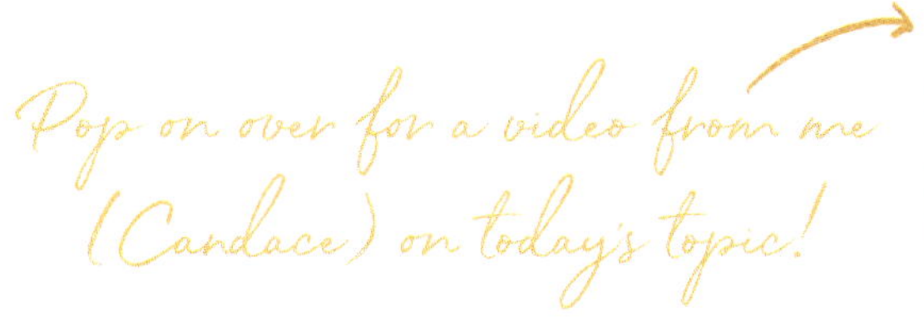

DAY 11

The Wait

Patient endurance is what you need now, so that you will continue to do God's will. Then you will receive all that He has promised.

HEBREWS 10:36

From the depths of despair, O Lord, I call for Your help. Hear my cry, O Lord. Pay attention to my prayer. . . . I am counting on the Lord; yes, I am counting on Him. I have put my hope in His word. I long for the Lord more than sentries long for the dawn, yes, more than sentries long for the dawn. O Israel, hope in the Lord; for with the Lord there is unfailing love. His redemption overflows (Psalm 130:1–2, 5–7).

Consider the farmers who patiently wait for the rains in the fall and in the spring. They eagerly look for the valuable harvest to ripen. You, too, must be patient. Take courage, for the coming of the Lord is near (James 5:7–8).

Let all that I am wait quietly before God, for my hope is in Him. He alone is my rock and my salvation, my fortress where I will not be shaken (Psalm 62:5–6).

Let us hold tightly without wavering to the hope we affirm, for God can be trusted to keep His promise (Hebrews 10:23).

We live by believing and not by seeing (II Corinthians 5:7).

This world is not our permanent home; we are looking forward to a home yet to come. Therefore, let us offer through Jesus a continual sacrifice of praise to God, proclaiming our allegiance to His name. And don't forget to do good and to share with those in need. These are the sacrifices that please God (Hebrews 13:14–16).

Patient endurance is what you need now, so that you will continue to do God's will. Then you will receive all that He has promised (Hebrews 10:36).

A NOTE FROM CANDACE

THE WAIT

Do you have a dream that feels like it's been put on hold? A longtime prayer that has yet to be answered? It could be anything: Starting a business. Getting married. Having a baby. Owning a home. Healing from an illness. Defeating an addiction.

Waiting is one of the hardest parts of being human, not to mention a huge cause of worry. Even if we know and believe that God has more for us than what we're seeing right now, it can get scary when there's no obvious forward movement. In the Bible, these are just a few of the "waits" that God's people endured:

- Abraham and Sarah waited twenty-five years for the son God had promised.
- Joseph was unjustly imprisoned for several years.
- The people of Israel trekked through the wilderness for forty years.
- The apostle Paul pleaded multiple times for God to relieve him of an affliction.

Tragically, the wait does a lot of people in. In the middle of worry moments, I've certainly tried to shortcut God's schedule. You too? Or sometimes I've wished so hard for the next thing that I've passed right by *this thing* that God is doing now.

These long waits are enough to make any of us ask, "Am I where I'm supposed to be? What am I missing?"

You may not be missing anything, friend. You may be in exactly the right place—while God is bringing other people and circumstances into alignment with His plan.

The important thing as we wait, writes pastor John Piper, is to place our trust in God's goodness, not in whether things go our way or follow our calendar. Piper describes it as "faith in future grace—the sovereign grace of God to turn the unplanned place and the unplanned pace"* into a far greater ending.

God is always on time.

In God's timing, the son born in Abraham and Sarah's old age fulfilled God's promise that Abraham would be the father of many nations—the patriarch of Christians everywhere.

In God's timing, Joseph was released from prison and appointed second-in-command in the most powerful nation on the planet, exactly at a time when he could prepare the ancient world (and his own family) for the worst effects of a seven-year famine.

In God's timing, the Israelites reached the Promised Land.

In God's timing, though the Lord chose not to remove Paul's affliction, He gave His servant more grace for the situation and more power in his weakness. Paul grew so sure of God, so content

* John Piper, *Future Grace: The Purifying Power of the Promises of God* (New York: Crown Publishing Group, 2012), 172.

in God, that he became practically unafraid of anything that his enemies or life itself could throw at him.

I have no idea how or when God may end your wait, or even if He will before you reach heaven. But I pray for your peace and comfort and an ever-increasing faith in this season.

You're not just waiting—you're waiting *on the Lord*.

THINK ON IT

What harvest are you waiting to reap someday?

Psalm 37:7–8 instructs:
"Be still before the Lord and wait patiently for Him. . . . do not fret—it leads only to evil" (NIV).
What negative effects have you experienced from your own impatience or someone else's?

THINK ON IT

Around the tenth year of what turned out to be a twenty-five-year wait for the son God promised, Sarah's faith wavered and she convinced Abraham to try for a child with her much younger servant. The servant did have a boy. But Sarah ended up despising the woman and the child.

In what situation have you chosen Sarah's approach, taking circumstances into your own hands in hopes of shortening the wait? What blessing did you miss (or almost miss) in that season?

David wrote that those who "delight in the law of the Lord, meditating on it day and night. . . . are like trees planted along the riverbank, bearing fruit each season. Their leaves never wither, and they prosper in all they do" (Psalm 1:1–3).

With God, even waiting seasons are growing seasons. How can you keep bearing fruit in this season? What disciplines and habits can you cultivate to weed out your worries?

Paul, who suffered greatly for his faith, encouraged fellow sufferers: "Let's not get tired of doing what is good. At just the right time we will reap a harvest of blessing if we don't give up" (Galatians 6:9). When you know you're going to reap in a later season, says Bible teacher Priscilla Shirer, "you will treat today differently." How will you handle today's circumstances, work, and relationships differently since a harvest is ahead?

ACT ON IT

Let's list three things we are currently waiting for in life, and then let's think through how much we are trusting God with these plans.

	FULLY	MOSTLY	SORT OF	NOT AT ALL
1.				
2.				
3.				

Pop on over for a video from me (Candace) on today's topic!

DAY 12

Heart Health

Now may the God of peace make you holy in every way, and may your whole spirit and soul and body be kept blameless until our Lord Jesus Christ comes again. God will make this happen, for He who calls you is faithful.

I THESSALONIANS 5:23–24

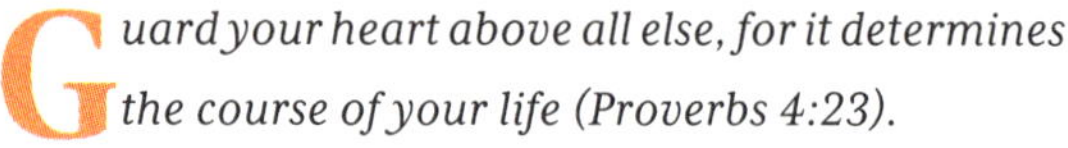

Guard your heart above all else, for it determines the course of your life (Proverbs 4:23).

Take hold of my instructions; don't let them go. Guard them, for they are the key to life. Don't do as the wicked do, and don't follow the path of evildoers. Don't even think about it; don't go that way. Turn away and keep moving (Proverbs 4:13–15).

My child, pay attention to what I say. Listen carefully to my words. Don't lose sight of them. Let them penetrate deep into your heart, for they bring life to those who find them, and healing to their whole body (Proverbs 4:20–22).

Don't worry about anything; instead, pray about everything. Tell God what you need, and thank Him for all He has done. Then you will experience God's peace, which exceeds anything we can understand. His peace will guard your hearts and minds as you live in Christ Jesus (Philippians 4:6–7).

Now may the God of peace make you holy in every way, and may your whole spirit and soul and body be kept blameless until our Lord Jesus Christ comes again. God will make this happen, for He who calls you is faithful (I Thessalonians 5:23–24).

I pray that your love will overflow more and more, and that you will keep on growing in knowledge and understanding. For I want you to understand what really matters, so that you may live pure and blameless lives until the day of Christ's return. May you always be filled with the fruit of your salvation—the righteous character produced in your life by Jesus Christ—for this will bring much glory and praise to God (Philippians 1:9–11).

A NOTE FROM CANDACE

HEART HEALTH

An acquaintance of mine had an ocular migraine for the first time earlier this year. Thinking it was a stroke, her mind went immediately to all the bad food choices she'd made in the previous month. That health scare prompted her to start eating more fruits and veggies from that day on, making smoothies a regular part of her diet.

It's such a simple idea, and yet it's spot-on: While eliminating unhealthy food from your diet is good for your health, what's even better is *replacing* the junk with nutritious alternatives before you encounter any warning signs. That's what gives your heart its best chance at a long life.

I want to be just as proactive in my spiritual life. I'd rather guard my heart by filling up on good daily habits than worry about playing defense once I'm "sick" with worry and regret. This approach not only strengthens my faith but puts me in a better position to remove threats quickly, before they become big problems.

You could call this God's healthcare plan. The entire idea originated with Him. Don't stop at getting rid of the junk nutritionally, emotionally, mentally, relationally, spiritually—fill that space with great, life-enhancing things before any bad stuff clogs your pipes.

- Instead of worrying, pray. Not alongside your worry, but in place of it.
- Don't just resist the devil; draw near to God.
- In place of vengeance, bless your enemies.
- Die to self so that you can live for God.

For Him to provide positive alternatives for His children is such a gift! God empowers us to become stronger, healthier—more whole and holy—in every area of our lives. Spiritually, this is called *sanctification*.

When you make Christ your Lord and Savior, He doesn't just remove sin; He begins to restore what's been broken and recover what's been lost so that your heart can become better than ever. Through the Holy Spirit, He also suggests further improvements for your faith and supplies all that you need for the work.

Satan doesn't ever offer or make improvements; he just empties more trash into our systems, creating a breeding ground for trouble. God, on the other hand, has created us so that a healthy heart brings us life and healing. In other words, ladies, that heart of yours is worth protecting. Guard it well.

THINK ON IT

Which health practices can you put into place to bring your anxiety levels down?

Which spiritual practices would help decrease your worry levels?

THINK ON IT

Our pasts are often a breeding ground for "heart disease." List a couple of the worries you've carried over from childhood or messages from past damaging choices that continue to plague you with feelings of shame or regret.

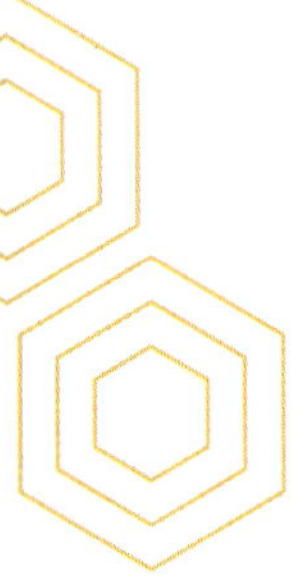

Thankfully, God knows how amazing you are, and He provides life-giving alternatives to those unhealthy messages! In Philippians 4:8 He reminds each of us: "Fix your thoughts on what is true, and honorable, and right, and pure, and lovely, and admirable. Think about things that are excellent and worthy of praise." Reply to each negative message you just listed with words that are true and lovely. For example, instead of "God could never forgive what I've done," write "God forgives and loves me no matter what I've done."

ACT ON IT

I had so much fun designing a line of T-shirts that communicates this idea of replacing the negative with God's best. Among those messages are

- Multiply kindness.
- Lift others up.
- Don't throw shade.
- Be kind.
- Love Over All.

Now it's your turn to get in on the fun. Design a couple of your own "instead" messages on the T-shirt templates below based on the Scriptures you've read or your answers to the last question in the Think On It section.

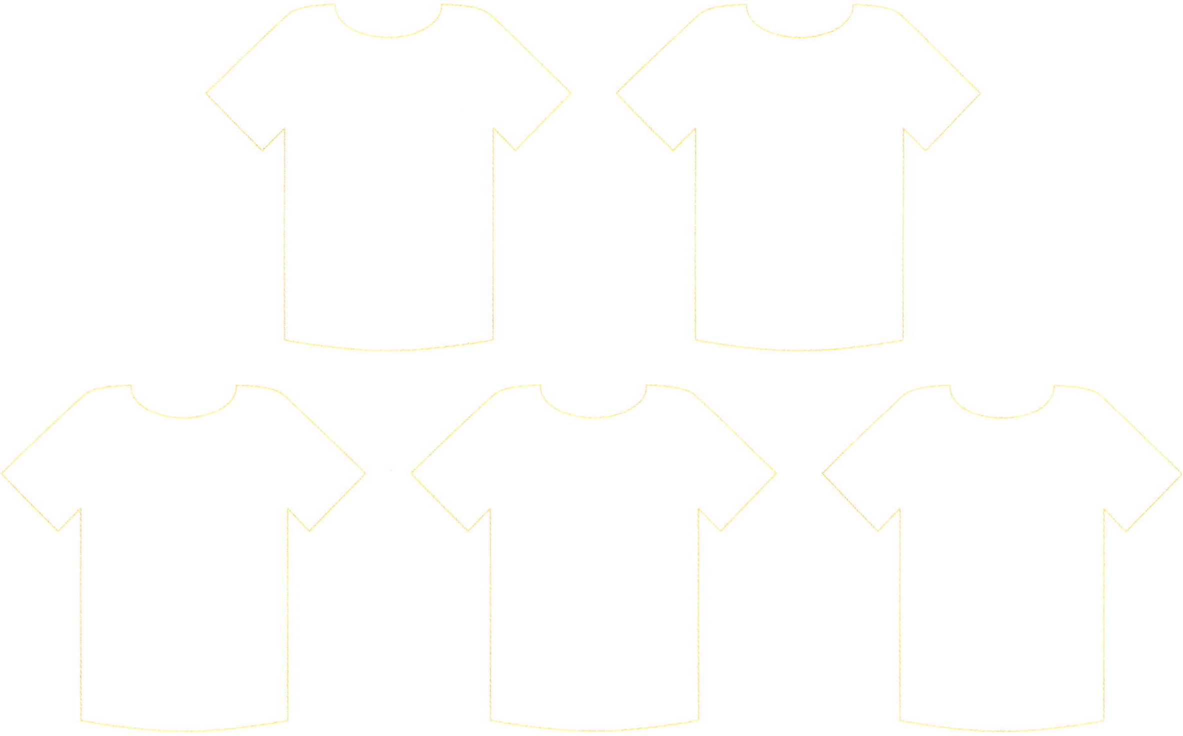

Pop on over for a video from me (Candace) on today's topic!

DAY 13

Full-Time Warrior

**Trust in the LORD
with all your heart;
do not depend
on your own understanding.
Seek His will in all you do,
and He will show you
which path to take.**

PROVERBS 3:5–6

Show me the right path, O LORD; point out the road for me to follow. . . . All day long I put my hope in You (Psalm 25:4–5).

You must love the LORD your God with all your heart, all your soul, all your mind, and all your strength (Mark 12:30).

Trust in the LORD with all your heart; do not depend on your own understanding. Seek His will in all you do, and He will show you which path to take (Proverbs 3:5–6).

Wash your hands, you sinners; purify your hearts, for your loyalty is divided between God and the world. Let there be tears for what you have done. Let there be sorrow and deep grief. . . . Humble yourselves before the Lord, and He will lift you up in honor (James 4:8–10).

Write this letter to the angel of the church in Laodicea. This is the message from the one who is the Amen—the faithful and true witness, the beginning of God's new creation:

"I know all the things you do, that you are neither hot nor cold. I wish that you were one or the other! But since you are like lukewarm water, neither hot nor cold, I will spit you out of my mouth! You say, 'I am rich. I have everything I want. I don't need a thing!' And you don't realize that you are wretched and miserable and poor and blind and naked. . . . I correct and discipline everyone I love. So be diligent and turn from your indifference" (Revelation 3:14–17, 19).

A NOTE FROM CANDACE

FULL-TIME WARRIOR

For a long time, especially in my young-adult years, I was more of a "foxhole Christian" than a full-time warrior. By that I mean I cried out to God when bombs were dropping; otherwise, our relationship was "courteous." A nice add-on but not essential.

King David often declared his faith, hope, and trust in God when he was under siege. But his wasn't a foxhole faith. He wasn't lukewarm toward God, ever. Or a lone ranger. He *trusted the Lord with all his heart*, and he *loved the Lord with all his heart*. Full-time, all in. Passionately devoted and permanently loyal—a true warrior.

How incredible would it be to be known as that kind of woman?

Making David's legacy our own starts with putting our hope in God "all day long." Steadfastly depending on God full-time—on good days and bad, with every step and every decision. How often do you put your hope in Him, really placing yourself in the Lord's hands? Only in emergencies? Only when you're scared or worried? Or from morning till night?

Something that strengthened my trust in God was learning to be specific in my prayers. I take all my concerns to Him—decisions, relationship issues, priorities or boundaries that need defining, attitudes I'm struggling with—and I ask Him to specifically show me His will. He might do that through His Word, through the counsel of others, through circumstances and "coincidences," or by bringing my heart and mind into agreement with His. Over and over, in ways I can't deny, He specifically guides my steps.

Besides David's enduring trust in the Lord, he devoted himself to the Lord, advising his son Solomon: "Learn to know the God of your ancestors intimately. Worship and serve Him with your whole heart and a willing mind. For the LORD sees every heart and knows every plan and thought. If you seek Him, you will find Him" (I Chronicles 28:9). Isn't that beautiful? Intimacy and trust, closeness and confidence—those relational seeds grow in time with time.

Passion + permanence was this warrior's secret to success. I promise you, a full-time, all-in relationship with God will grow your reliance on Him, your love for Him, and your confidence in Him. It will also help you let go of all your worries and fears, producing a resilience in you for the battles you'll face, exactly as it did for David.

Let's not be part-time believers. Let's opt out of the courtesies and the crisis-only cries for help and choose deep, lasting companionship. Second Chronicles 16:9 assures every warrior of this: "The eyes of the LORD search the whole earth in order to strengthen those whose hearts are fully committed to Him."

THINK ON IT

Evaluate yourself: How much do you rely on God in your day-to-day life? How passionately do you pursue Him?

How do you specifically exhibit your love for Him and your trust in Him?

How could a greater reliance on God erase more of your daily worry and fear?

THINK ON IT

How can you become more permanent—more steadfast and consistent—with your trust in God? Be specific.

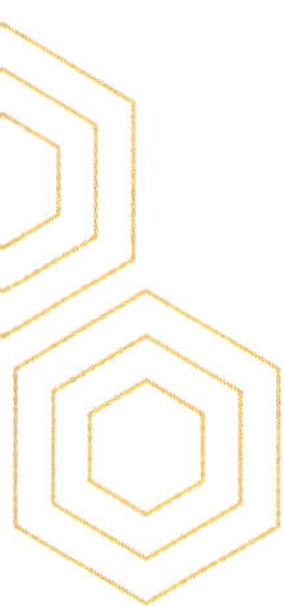

What difference would this kind of trust make in the things you persistently struggle with?

What would encourage your love for God? Think of what you do to deepen your bonds in your closest human relationships and then list a few ways you could likewise develop your relationship with God.

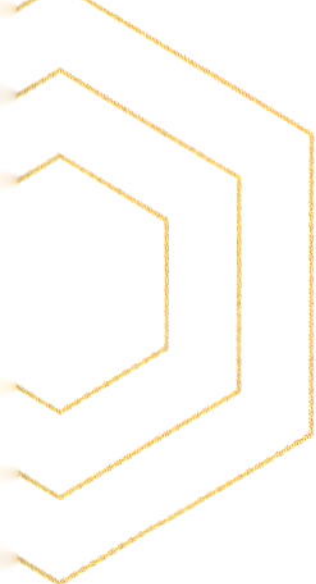

ACT ON IT

To me, putting my hope in God all day long is more than prayer and Bible reading. It includes the practices and type of relationship building that David included in Psalm 86. Using different-colored pencils, highlighters, or ink pens, mark each way that David exemplified or encouraged both a passionate *and* a steadfast devotion to the Lord. Make notes to yourself in the margins as additional thoughts come to you.

O Lord . . . hear my prayer;
answer me, for I need Your help.
Protect me, for I am devoted to You.
Save me, for I serve You and trust You.
You are my God.
Be merciful to me, O Lord,
for I am calling on You constantly.
Give me happiness, O Lord,
for I give myself to You.
O Lord, You are so good, so ready to forgive,
so full of unfailing love for all who ask for Your help.
Listen closely to my prayer, O Lord;
hear my urgent cry.
I will call to You whenever I'm in trouble,
and You will answer me. . . .

For You are great and perform wonderful deeds.
You alone are God.

Teach me Your ways, O Lord,
that I may live according to Your truth!
Grant me purity of heart,
so that I may honor You.
With all my heart I will praise You, O Lord my God.
I will give glory to Your name forever,
for Your love for me is very great.

(VERSES 1-7, 10-13)

Pop on over for a video from me (Candace) on today's topic!

DAY 14

Laying Hold of Happiness

Seek the Kingdom of God above all else, and He will give you everything you need.... Don't be afraid, little flock. For it gives your Father great happiness to give you the Kingdom.

LUKE 12:31–32

Whatever is good and perfect is a gift coming down to us from God our Father, who created all the lights in the heavens. He never changes or casts a shifting shadow. He chose to give birth to us by giving us His true word. And we, out of all creation, became His prized possession (James 1:17–18).

The LORD your God is living among you. He is a mighty savior. He will take delight in you with gladness. With His love, He will calm all your fears. He will rejoice over you with joyful songs (Zephaniah 3:17).

Give me happiness, O Lord, for I give myself to You (Psalm 86:4).

Seek the Kingdom of God above all else, and He will give you everything you need. . . . Don't be afraid, little flock. For it gives your Father great happiness to give you the Kingdom (Luke 12:31–32).

"You parents—if your children ask for a loaf of bread, do you give them a stone instead? Or if they ask for a fish, do you give them a snake? Of course not! So if you sinful people know how to give good gifts to your children, how much more will your heavenly Father give good gifts to those who ask Him" (Matthew 7:9–11).

A NOTE FROM CANDACE

LAYING HOLD OF HAPPINESS

If you're a lover of great stories like I am, you've probably read some of Jane Austen's novels or seen them on the big screen. *Pride and Prejudice*, *Sense and Sensibility*, and *Emma* are some of her best-known works. She also wrote *Northanger Abbey*, and in that book one of her characters offers what I think is some pretty great advice: "It is well to have as many holds upon happiness as possible."

I'm all for lots of happiness! Concentrating on the things that bring us joy can take our minds off worrying about the things that could happen. It's like bringing home a huge bouquet of flowers every morning from the neighborhood florist or farmers' market. Each bouquet, hand-picked for you, comes courtesy of the One who cherishes you with a tenderness and affection that He can't hold back. Every happiness in your day is sent with love, from Him.

Here are some of the simpler touches that make my bouquet full:

- The soothing comfort of a hot cup of coffee or tea first thing in the morning
- My husband, after twenty-five years of marriage, still wanting to hold my hand when we go out
- The glow of a hard workout (the working out doesn't always make me happy, but I sure do like the aftereffects!)
- Having the perfect shade of lipstick and the right shoes to accent my outfit
- Getting a hug or a call from one of my grown kids
- A candlelit bubble bath after a long, hard week
- Being able to blast my favorite music in my car, where I can sing as loudly as my inner sixteen-year-old self wants to
- A couple scoops of mint chocolate chip ice cream to top off a fun dinner out with the girls
- Enjoying fresh air, sunshine, and the beauty of nature

These kinds of happinesses brighten my day. Their fragrance and beauty help to clear my mind of worry and stress. How about you?

You, too, can lay hold of a bundle of happiness, starting with all those good gifts that God sends from heaven. But let's never forget the Giver. He is the true prize in all of this. With a love that is unchanging and unconditional, our Daddy in heaven claims us proudly as His own, His beloved, His daughters. That's not only cause for happiness, ladies; that's a reason for no fear!

THINK ON IT

What was the best gift you ever received? How did it make you feel?

Why did it mean so much to you?

List two or three eternal gifts God has given you that are especially valuable to you. How does each of those gifts make you feel? Why do they mean so much to you?

THINK ON IT

What do God's material and spiritual gifts say about His heart for you? If He loves you enough to give you these gifts, how do you think He wants you to view your worries?

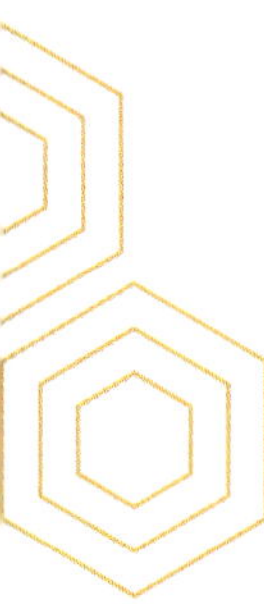

Think about the passage from Matthew 7:9–11 on the Scripture page.
What does it mean to be God's beloved daughter?
If you're a mom, how can you relate your parental love for your children to God's love for you?

What would you like to say to the Giver?

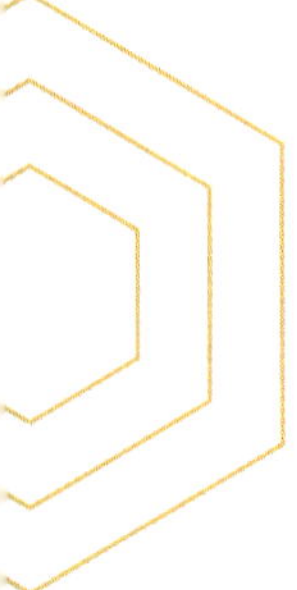

ACT ON IT

There's a traditional church hymn that begins with these words: "Count your blessings, name them one by one." Our Father in heaven lovingly offers each of His daughters a fresh array of day-brightening blessings to choose from. His "mix" combines brilliant colors and subtle shades with smaller, delicate accents—all of them delivered from His garden to our hearts.

So what's in *your* bouquet today? We've prepared an array of flowers—an array of blessings—for you to label and color one by one. You can also draw more if you'd like, making an even fuller bouquet.

As you enjoy your flowers, open your heart to God and let Him sing over you with love.

Pop on over for a video from me (Candace) on today's topic!

DAY 15

Dust

O LORD,
You are our Father.
We are the clay,
and You are the potter.
We all are formed
by Your hand.

ISAIAH 64:8

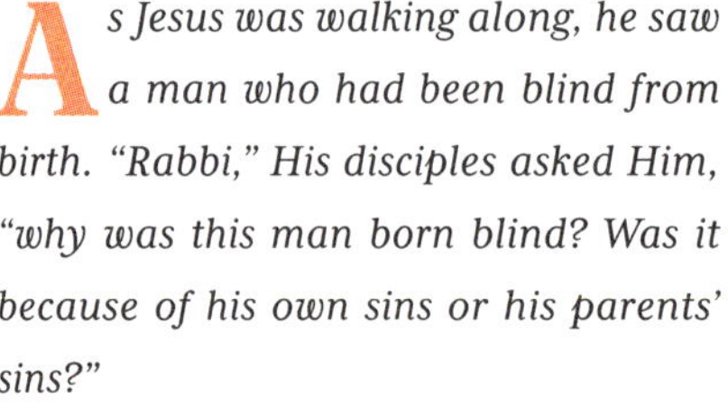

As Jesus was walking along, he saw a man who had been blind from birth. "Rabbi," His disciples asked Him, "why was this man born blind? Was it because of his own sins or his parents' sins?"

"It was not because of his sins or his parents' sins," Jesus answered. "This happened so the power of God could be seen in him. . . . While I am here in the world, I am the light of the world."

Then He spit on the ground, made mud with the saliva, and spread the mud over the blind man's eyes. He told him, "Go wash yourself in the pool of Siloam" . . . So the man went and washed and came back seeing! (John 9:1–3, 5–7)

O LORD, You are our Father. We are the clay, and You are the potter. We all are formed by Your hand (Isaiah 64:8).

To all who mourn in Israel, He will give a crown of beauty for ashes, a joyous blessing instead of mourning, festive praise instead of despair. In their righteousness, they will be like great oaks that the Lord *has planted for His own glory (Isaiah 61:3).*

[The Lord] knows how weak we are; He remembers we are only dust (Psalm 103:14).

In a wealthy home some utensils are made of gold and silver, and some are made of wood and clay. The expensive utensils are used for special occasions, and the cheap ones are for everyday use. If you keep yourself pure, you will be a special utensil for honorable use. Your life will be clean, and you will be ready for the Master to use you for every good work (II Timothy 2:20–21).

A NOTE FROM CANDACE

DUST

In one of Jesus' miracles, He declared Himself "the light of the world," and then proved He was by healing a man who had been born blind.

His method in this instance—spitting on the ground to make mud and applying it to the man's eyes—wouldn't be my preference, though my sons, Lev and Maks, might think it's a pretty cool way to make the point. Regardless, I sure wouldn't argue with that approach if it meant getting that kind of result.

This was just one of Jesus' many ways of illustrating God's ability to produce beauty from the ashes of our lives. I think we could all use some of that right now, don't you? Every year people lose loved ones or jobs. Every year marriages fail and friendships shatter. Every year people face financial hardships, infertility, or jobs that feel like a prison sentence. Life on planet earth is tough.

In soul-crushing times, we'd give just about anything for God to fix it, writes best-selling author Lysa TerKeurst in her powerful book *It's Not Supposed to Be This Way*: "Edit this story so it has a different ending. Repair this heartbreaking reality."* But what if all that fixing isn't "what God has in mind . . . ? What if, this time, God desires to make something completely brand-new?"*

Jesus, the Living Water, may decide to heal those losses using the dust we're sitting in. Or the Lord our Father—the divine Potter—may decide to create an entirely new work from the dust we're made of. Either way, our Creator is not sitting idle. As Lysa so beautifully reminds us, "When mixed with water, dust becomes clay. Clay, when placed in the potter's hands, can be formed into anything the potter dreams up! . . . Dust doesn't have to signify the end," she says. "Dust is often what must be present for the new to begin."**

If you've suffered a loss that has left your life in ashes, tender warrior, what God is doing with it can be the least of your worries. He is doing *something*. And though you probably don't feel it right now, He is *for you*, not against you. Whether He decides to cast a brand-new mold or to repair the breaks, your dust is in His hands. Trust Him.

---

* Lisa TerKeurst, *It's Not Supposed to Be This Way: Finding Unexpected Strength When Disappointments Leave You Shattered* (Nashville: Thomas Nelson, 2018), 17.

** Ibid., 18.

THINK ON IT

Where do you feel broken right now? What loss do you need to recover from? (It might be from years ago, or it could be current.)

How are you doing in this season?

What's your view of God as you're covered in dust?

THINK ON IT

The apostle Paul wrote, "My old self has been crucified with Christ. It is no longer I who live, but Christ lives in me. So I live in this earthly body by trusting in the Son of God, who loved me and gave Himself for me" (Galatians 2:19–20). What evidence have you seen that Christ is at work in your life—reshaping, restoring, rebuilding, resurrecting your new self?

In what ways are you allowing the divine Potter to remold your thoughts or attitudes?

How prone are you to getting in His way? Are you trying to control what He does with your dust? Reread the II Timothy 2 passage on the Scripture page. How can you "keep yourself pure" in your situation?

ACT ON IT

When Jesus was praying in the Garden of Gethsemane before His crucifixion, He was in agony thinking about the suffering He was about to experience. Nevertheless, Jesus put Himself in God's hands, praying, "My Father! If it is possible, let this cup of suffering be taken away from Me. Yet I want Your will to be done, not Mine" (Matthew 26:39).

Entrusting yourself to the Master Potter is never easy. I encourage you, though, to bring your questions and fears to God through it all.

For this exercise, search your heart and express your desires for what God will do with these ashes of yours. List those in the first section below. Next—if you're ready—write a prayer of surrender to Him. (If you're not there yet, just admitting your wishes can be a prayer of its own.)

Confess your worries about the refining process. Share what you hope for and what you feel you need. Then hold this page open in your two hands and lift them to heaven as a gesture that you are entrusting yourself and all the "dust" into His care. Close this time of prayer with Jesus' own words of surrender: "Father . . . I want Your will to be done, not Mine."

MY WISHES

MY PRAYER

Pop on over for a video from me (Candace) on today's topic!

DAY 16

Build Your Army

Let us think of ways to motivate one another to acts of love and good works. And let us not neglect our meeting together, as some people do, but encourage one another, especially now that the day of His return is drawing near.

HEBREWS 10:24–25

Two people are better off than one, for they can help each other succeed. If one person falls, the other can reach out and help. But someone who falls alone is in real trouble. Likewise . . . a person standing alone can be attacked and defeated, but two can stand back-to-back and conquer. Three are even better, for a triple-braided cord is not easily broken (Ecclesiastes 4:9–12).

Share each other's burdens, and in this way obey the law of Christ (Galatians 6:2).

Is there any encouragement from belonging to Christ? Any comfort from His love? Any fellowship together in the Spirit? Are your hearts tender and compassionate? Then make me truly happy by agreeing wholeheartedly with each other, loving one another, and working together with one mind and purpose (Philippians 2:1–2).

As iron sharpens iron, so a friend sharpens a friend (Proverbs 27:17).

Let us think of ways to motivate one another to acts of love and good works. And let us not neglect our meeting together, as some people do, but encourage one another, especially now that the day of His return is drawing near (Hebrews 10:24–25).

[While Joshua and his men fought the army of Amalek,] Moses, Aaron, and Hur climbed to the top of a nearby hill. As long as Moses held up the staff in his hand, the Israelites had the advantage. But whenever he dropped his hand, the Amalekites gained the advantage. Moses' arms soon became so tired he could no longer hold them up. So Aaron and Hur found a stone for him to sit on. Then they stood on each side of Moses, holding up his hands. So his hands held steady until sunset. As a result, Joshua overwhelmed the army of Amalek in battle (Exodus 17:10–13).

A NOTE FROM CANDACE

BUILD YOUR ARMY

As much as we might prefer to make things happen on our own, friends, it's not healthy for us to do life alone, without other women. Satan is all for isolation. That's how the lion in the jungle chooses his victims. He looks for the creature that's a little removed from the group. He singles out the one that's not surrounded by the herd.

I'll tell you right now, that won't be me! If the enemy is going to come after me, he'll have to get past my squadron, which isn't easy! I have an army of women around me who look out for me, defend me, encourage me, pray for me, challenge me, and believe in me. Each individual is another layer of protection from attack, from temptation, from loneliness, and even from worry.

These women certainly don't all look like me or think like me. That diversity is part of the strength of this tribe. Dilini, my best friend since high school, is a Buddhist. Yet she's one of the captains of my team because she knows me and loves me and wants to see me become my best. My sisters and my mom are part of my tribe as well. I'm also grateful for the study groups and prayer groups I've been able to be part of through church.

My friend Stacy was the first person to ever ask me to be accountable as a prayer partner—where we regularly shared our prayer requests (and God's answers) with each other and committed to praying consistently for each other. It came at a good time in my life because I was wondering, "How should I pray? Where do I learn?"

Through praying with others, I realized there's something wonderful about knowing someone's got your back—where they're in the trenches fighting alongside you spiritually. Seeing *their* prayers answered, too, has strengthened my confidence in God.

For each of us, that army of friends and family is one of God's best resources for building up our faith and ensuring that we succeed in the things God has called us to. I love what Jesus says in Matthew 18:19-20: "If two of you agree here on earth concerning anything you ask, My Father in heaven will do it for you. For where two or three gather together as My followers, I am there among them."

That's the power of the pack, ladies! Don't you dare try to go it alone!

THINK ON IT

What are the most critical roles that your army plays in your daily life?

Why is it important to have friends of different ages?

How many "generations" of friends do you have?

THINK ON IT

During Israel's battle with the Amalekites (see the Exodus 17 passage on the Scripture page), the Lord commanded Moses to pray and keep his staff raised to symbolize the army's need for God. When Moses' arms grew tired, his brother, Aaron, and a friend, Hur, stepped in to further support him. In what similar ways have your friends upheld you when you were growing weary during a battle? Who needs you to be an Aaron or Hur for them right now?

Titus 2 instructs older women to mentor younger women. What traits would you want a mentor to have? Who are the older women in your life with those qualities? Write out your action plan for befriending them.

No matter your age, there are younger women you could befriend and possibly mentor. What steps could you take to build relationships with them?

ACT ON IT

Every one of us sometimes carries worry with us without knowing it. Whether it's a small thought that follows you throughout the day or a crippling fear that stops you in your tracks, who is your Aaron? Your Hur? Who are the folks you can call when you're fighting a battle or when you're worried and can't sleep?

Make a plan by writing the names of those warriors below. Then thank each one for standing in the gap for you with a personalized thank-you note.

Consider including this Bible passage on a separate piece of card stock:

> *Every time I think of you, I give thanks to my God. Whenever I pray, I make my requests for all of you with joy, for you have been my partners in spreading the Good News about Christ from the time you first heard it until now. And I am certain that God, who began the good work within you, will continue His work until it is finally finished on the day when Christ Jesus returns (Philippians 1:3–6).*

You could design it on the computer and print it, or write it in a beautiful script, or ask an artistic friend to do it for you.

When you mail out these notes, say a prayer for each person, asking the Lord to bless her and to continue to build up her army too. Fill in the star beside each name when you're done.

☆ NAME ______________________

☆ NAME ______________________

☆ NAME ______________________

☆ NAME ______________________

☆ NAME ______________________

☆ NAME ______________________

☆ NAME ______________________

☆ NAME ______________________

☆ NAME ______________________

DAY 17

No Shame in Small

**I alone am God! I am God,
and there is none like Me.
Only I can tell you the future
before it even happens.
Everything I plan will come to pass,
for I do whatever I wish.**

ISAIAH 46:9–10

Jesus sat down near the collection box in the Temple and watched as the crowds dropped in their money. Many rich people put in large amounts. Then a poor widow came and dropped in two small coins.

Jesus called His disciples to Him and said, "I tell you the truth, this poor widow has given more than all the others who are making contributions. For they gave a tiny part of their surplus, but she, poor as she is, has given everything she had to live on" (Mark 12:41–44).

My dear brothers and sisters, be strong and immovable. Always work enthusiastically for the Lord, for you know that nothing you do for the Lord is ever useless (I Corinthians 15:58).

Another message came to me from the Lord*: "Zerubabbel is the one who laid the foundation of this Temple, and he will complete it. Then you will know that the* Lord *of Heaven's Armies has sent Me. Do not despise these small beginnings, for the* Lord *rejoices to see the work begin, to see the plumb line in [the governor's] hand" (Zechariah 4:8–10).*

"I alone am God! I am God, and there is none like Me. Only I can tell you the future before it even happens. Everything I plan will come to pass, for I do whatever I wish" (Isaiah 46:9–10).

A NOTE FROM CANDACE

NO SHAME IN SMALL

When Jesus spoke of the kingdom of God, He sometimes used images of small things: a sprinkling of salt that preserves a large slab of meat, a pinch of yeast that spreads through an entire loaf of bread and allows it to rise, the smallest seed in the garden growing into a great tree where the birds can nest.

These parables remind me that in God's eyes there is no such thing as too small. When blessed by Him, small things continually foreshadowed great things in Scripture:

- From the line of Israel's smallest tribe (Benjamin) came two of the most important figures in Bible history—the apostle Paul and Esther.
- From a little town named Bethlehem came a tiny baby who would change the world.
- From the ministry of a few apostles, the Christian church expanded to every continent on earth.

Jesus affirmed this when He pointed to the widow in the temple giving the two coins she owned to the Lord, and He told His disciples that her offering was the greatest of them all because she gave her all, willingly.

I don't know about you, but as a woman with a lot of big dreams and plans, I need that reminder sometimes. I can get impatient at small starts. I find myself worrying that nothing will come of them. The servant of the Lord said as much in Isaiah 49: "My work seems so useless! I have spent my strength for nothing and to no purpose" (verse 4).

Maybe you've had a few of those situations yourself. Maybe you're looking at one right now and thinking, *This is such an uninspiring beginning that it can't possibly be anything for God.*

We can make that mistake with seemingly small tasks, small sacrifices, small callings. Yet whether our call is to a new business, a ministry, or a simple act of service, we can give it our all for the Lord and watch what He does.

I know, I know. The world likes for us to go big, and if we don't, we're supposed to go home. But Zechariah 4 reminds us to never minimize small beginnings. The eyes of the Lord see past what catches people's eye.

When we give our all, our sovereign God doesn't care if it's small. He is able to make it as big as He wants it, grow it as wide or as deep as He decides. Stay faithful. He'll size it as He sees fit, and He will turn your sacrifice into a sweet offering that blesses Him, blesses you, and blesses others.

THINK ON IT

When have you seen something small become something great or act in a powerful way? What effect did the sight of that have on you?

Isaiah 46:9–10 on the Scripture page is a call not to passivity but to confidence, humility, and reverence. What assurance can you take in these words of the Lord if He sizes things smaller than you hoped? What if He upsizes beyond your imagination?

THINK ON IT

The servant finishes his statement in Isaiah 49:4 with the words: "Yet I leave it all in the LORD's hand; I will trust God for my reward." How easy or difficult is this level of trust for you with your small offering? Why?

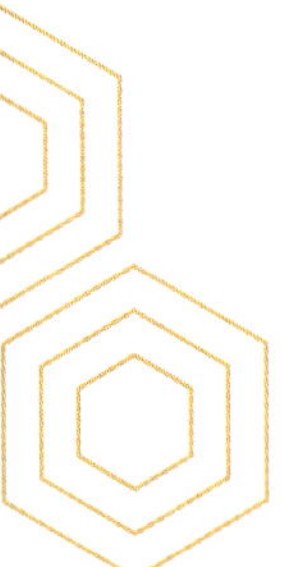

First Corinthians 15:58 promises that our work in God's name is never in vain. Isaiah 46:10 assures us that God's plans "come to pass." How does His faithfulness to you and to His outcomes strengthen your outlook? Your efforts?

Reread the passage from Zechariah 4. The Lord promised that those who were ashamed of the size of the house of worship that was being built would one day rejoice when they saw the governor of Judah (Zerubbabel) checking the finished building with the plumb line. However, we don't have to wait to rejoice. What "small" victories are you witnessing already in the things the Lord has called you to?

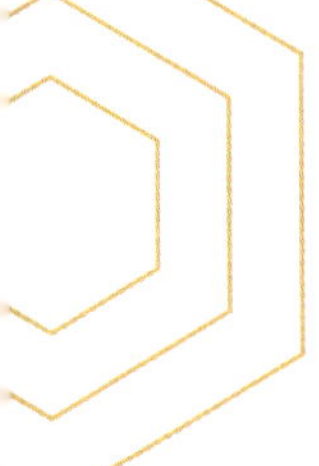

ACT ON IT

In Proverbs 30:24–28, the biblical writer mentions a few creatures in nature that "are small but unusually wise: Ants—they aren't strong, but they store up food all summer. . . . Locusts—they have no king, but they march in formation. Lizards—they are easy to catch, but they are found even in kings' palaces."

Take a look around you. What small but mighty things do you see or use that you normally don't even think about but that ease your worries or make your life easier? For the next few days, note those little things below. As you compile your list, pause and thank God for the usefulness or beauty of each item. What would your life be without these objects?

Expand your list by noting any small steps of progress in your habits. Also highlight the small deeds you see others doing or the little things others do for you. Proverbs 11:30 reminds us: "The seeds of good deeds become a tree of life." And last but not least, write down the glimmers of truth and hope that God gives you to relieve your fears and encourage you in your journey with Him. Those encouragements could come from words you hear, words you read, or answers to prayer.

MY FAVORITE "LITTLE" THINGS

Pop on over for a video from me (Candace) on today's topic!

DAY 18

Keep It Clean

If you, LORD,
kept a record of sins,
Lord, who could stand?
But with You there is forgiveness,
so that we can, with reverence,
serve You.

PSALM 130:3–4 NIV

If we claim we have no sin, we are only fooling ourselves and not living in the truth. But if we confess our sins to [God], He is faithful and just to forgive us our sins and to cleanse us from all wickedness (I John 1:8–9).

People who conceal their sins will not prosper, but if they confess and turn from them, they will receive mercy (Proverbs 28:13).

You desire honesty from the womb, teaching me wisdom even there. . . . Purify me from my sins, and I will be clean; wash me, and I will be whiter than snow. Oh, give me back my joy again; You have broken me—now let me rejoice. Don't keep looking at my sins. Remove the stain of my guilt. Create in me a clean heart, O God. Renew a loyal spirit within me (Psalm 51:6–10).

Oh, what joy for those whose disobedience is forgiven, whose sin is put out of sight! Yes, what joy for those whose record the Lord has cleared of guilt, whose lives are lived in complete honesty! (Psalm 32:1–2)

If you, Lord, kept a record of sins, Lord, who could stand? But with You there is forgiveness, so that we can, with reverence, serve You (Psalm 130:3–4 NIV).

A NOTE FROM CANDACE

KEEP IT CLEAN

Everybody has one, don't they—a junk drawer where they toss all their random stuff until "someday" when they can get to it? Or a jam-packed closet or storage unit somewhere?

We're careful not to let company see those hideaways. I've even heard of people putting their dirty dishes in the shower until their guests have left! It doesn't matter—out of sight isn't out of mind. *We* know the mess is there, and that awareness weighs us down. Enough that numerous studies have shown a direct connection between decluttering and losing weight. Typically, those who purge their junk drop some pounds as well.

It's so much better to follow the advice of professional home organizers: Clean up your spaces, and then keep them clean as you go. Put your groceries away as soon as you get them. Handle any mail or paperwork only once. Rehang your clothes or drop them in the laundry at bedtime. That way, you're maintaining. Daily maintenance is much easier on the body and soul than digging out from under a pile you've been creating for years.

God similarly commands us to keep a clean slate before Him and with others. Repent of your sins when you sin, not six months later. Don't go to bed angry. Admit your worries and fears rather than denying them. Slam the door on temptation completely—don't give Satan a foothold by tolerating just "a little" sin.

It's not because the Lord is mean that He wants you to maintain cleanliness; it's because He's a holy God who also happens to wholeheartedly love you. When you fail to "declutter," it restricts your relationship with Him (and often with others). That mess, just like a pile of junk, becomes a barrier, preventing peace.

Ultimately, in the same way that your clutter weighs you down, so does the stuff you don't admit to. But "keeping current" and clearing out the junk daily, including your worries and fears, makes every warrior ready to be used by God anytime, anywhere.

THINK ON IT

When was the last time you decluttered a space in your home such as a closet, a desk, or a garage? How did that feel once it was finished?

David admitted to God, "Against You, and You alone, have I sinned; I have done what is evil in Your sight" (Psalm 51:4). These are called "private sins"—we aren't sinning against anyone but the Lord. How does naming our private sins help us let go of worry?

THINK ON IT

God has good reason for commanding urgency toward sin. Here's how David experienced delayed repentance: "When I refused to confess my sin, my body wasted away, and I groaned all day long. Day and night Your hand of discipline was heavy on me. My strength evaporated like water in the summer heat. Finally, I confessed all my sins to You and stopped trying to hide my guilt. . . . And You forgave me! All my guilt is gone" (Psalm 32:3–5). List the variety of effects we can suffer by putting off repentance. What have you experienced personally? Remember, repentance is not only confessing sin and asking for forgiveness, it is also turning away from that sin, as if you were turning your car 180 degrees to go the other way.

James 5:16 instructs, "Confess your sins to each other and pray for each other so that you may be healed." How do you feel about confessing things to God? To those you have wronged? Who is easier for you to ask for forgiveness? Why?

Rather than worrying over any guilt or sin, let it go right now. What's cluttering up your mind or heart? What unresolved relationship issues or unconfessed sins are weighing you down and preventing peace?

ACT ON IT

You can probably guess what this exercise is going to be. That's right—set aside a couple hours in your schedule to clear out a space that's become cluttered. We all have them, so don't feel any shame, and don't judge yourself for it. I promise, you'll be so glad you tackled it, and you'll be really proud of yourself too!

I'd recommend starting small, with a junk drawer or closet. Be sure to have a trash bag handy for the throwaways, a couple of boxes for the stuff you want to donate, and a bin for further action like returning things you've borrowed from others or putting back the things that belong in different spaces.

Once you've finished with that task, come back to this page. . . .

The process you went through physically to clean out your space is a picture of what you can do spiritually to clean your slate. Prayerfully think about your relationships, the feelings you've been denying, and the sins you may be hiding. Put each one in its proper category and then handle each pile accordingly.

TRASH

What do I need to get rid of?

- Sins ______________________
- Bad habits ______________________
- Temptations ______________________
- Lies ______________________
- Worries ______________________
- Anger ______________________

DONATE

What do I need to give to someone else?

- Burdens (to God) ______________________
- Forgiveness ______________________
- Grace ______________________
- Help ______________________
- Tasks or responsibilities (to their rightful owners) ______________________

FINISH

What I have left undone?

- Repair a relationship ______________________
- Resolve my issues ______________________
- Complete open tasks ______________________
- Address fears ______________________
- Establish boundaries ______________________

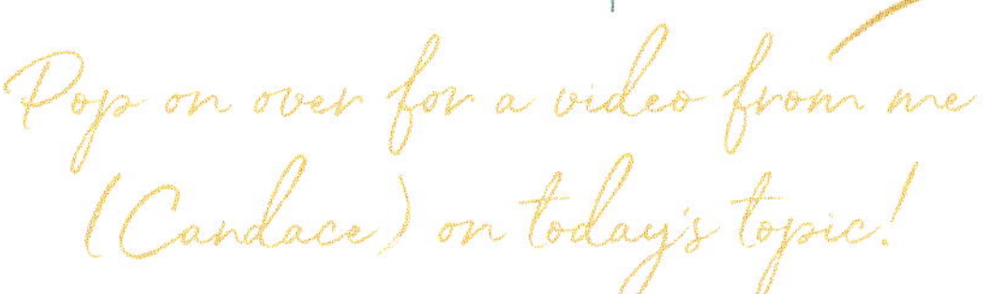

At Least Ask

**God has said,
"I will never fail you.
I will never abandon you."
So we can say with confidence,
"The LORD is my helper,
so I will have no fear."**

HEBREWS 13:5–6

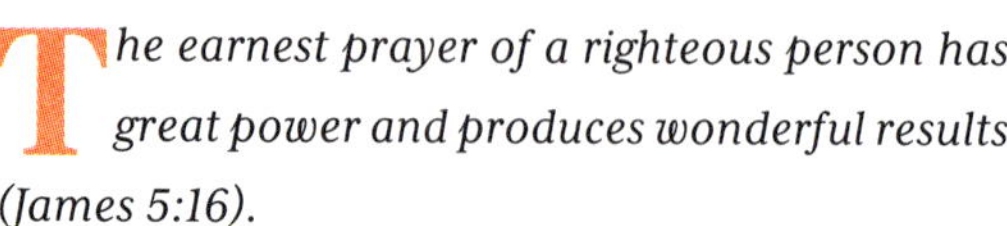

The earnest prayer of a righteous person has great power and produces wonderful results (James 5:16).

This is the confidence we have in approaching God: that if we ask anything according to His will, He hears us. And if we know that He hears us—whatever we ask—we know that we have what we asked of Him (I John 5:14–15 NIV).

O Lord, You know all about this. Do not stay silent. Do not abandon me now, O Lord. Wake up! Rise to my defense! Take up my case, my God and my Lord (Psalm 35:22–23).

God has said, "I will never fail you. I will never abandon you." So we can say with confidence, "The Lord is my helper, so I will have no fear." (Hebrews 13:5–6)

Now all glory to God, who is able, through His mighty power at work within us, to accomplish infinitely more than we might ask or think (Ephesians 3:20).

A NOTE FROM CANDACE

AT LEAST ASK

When he was young, my son Lev had two surgeries for a life-threatening tumor in his right ear. After the second surgery, doctors scheduled a CT scan to confirm that the tumor was gone. On the day of the test, I called the surgeon's office: "We have the disk. How soon can the doctor review the results?"

The receptionist replied that the doctor was leaving for a month-long trip overseas that night. We could get a pathology report once he was back, she offered.

When I heard it would be a month, I pleaded for my son. I told the receptionist I could come to the doctor's office *this afternoon*. The woman was sympathetic, but their office was closing at four, and there weren't any openings. I looked at the clock. It was 2:30.

"I understand," I said, "but would the doctor see me if I show up? Can he fit me in just for the few minutes it would take to look at the scan?"

The receptionist said I could try.

For the entire hour-long drive through Miami, I prayed for God to please, please get me through the traffic and get me in front of that surgeon.

At his office building I saw a crowd outside the entrance. "Fire alarm," they said. Soon, security reported that it had been a false alarm—burnt popcorn in a microwave—and everyone could return to the building.

I hurried inside and headed straight to our doctor's floor. Nobody was in the waiting room, but I could hear voices in the exam area. After a few minutes, I opened the door to see if I could talk to someone. At that moment Lev's doctor turned the corner.

I explained our situation, and asked, "Is there any way you could give me his results today, before you leave for vacation?" Since none of his scheduled patients were around, the doctor agreed to take a look. Lev's scans were clear.

That moment took my breath away. Honestly, it still does. Who knew that burnt popcorn could ever be God's perfectly timed answer to prayer?

I read the words of James 4:2 differently now: "You don't have what you want because you don't ask God for it." What if I hadn't asked the receptionist if I could come on in? What if I hadn't checked the exam area and asked the doctor to take a look at the scan?

What if I hadn't asked the Lord to intervene?

Is God in every detail? Absolutely! So ask, prayer warriors. Ask God to work through others and through your circumstances for what you need. You just never know—you may witness a miracle.

THINK ON IT

What's the craziest answer to prayer you've ever received?

When have you watched God "clear a path" for you at a time when you really needed it? What obstacles did He remove that you never could have eliminated for yourself?

THINK ON IT

Do you have a huge ask that you're afraid to share with God? If so, what past experience—perhaps with a parent or a boss—do you picture that keeps you from asking?

Think of a circumstance when you needed a favor, you asked, and the person was glad to help. Maybe you were at the grocery store or on an airplane or waiting in line somewhere. Describe your feelings in that moment, at both asking and receiving. Now think of God in that person's place. He is eager to come to your aid.

ACT ON IT

Romans 4 says this about Abraham's faith in God's promise to give him a son in his old age:

> *Even when there was no reason for hope, Abraham kept hoping—believing that he would become the father of many nations. For God had said to him, "That's how many descendants you will have!" And Abraham's faith did not weaken, even though, at about 100 years of age, he figured his body was as good as dead—and so was Sarah's womb.*
>
> *Abraham never wavered in believing God's promise. In fact, his faith grew stronger, and in this he brought glory to God. He was fully convinced that God is able to do whatever he promises. And because of Abraham's faith, God counted him as righteous. (verses 18–22).*

Obviously, not every promise in Scripture applies to us. Some, like this one, are specific to individuals or a time in history. Nevertheless, aspects of Abraham's faith are transferable to our lives. In each of the imprints below, write some of the ways you can "follow in his footsteps" from the passage above (we've given you an example for starters), and then add any others that come to mind for the circumstancs you're facing. Then, write down your wildest prayer request. Include your fears and hesitations, but also affirm your convictions about who God is and what He is capable of doing.

God knows your heart. Give yourself the freedom to express your desire, and sign it and date it so you have record of it.

PRAYER REQUEST

Pop on over for a video from me (Candace) on today's topic!

Protected

**As for me,
how good it is to be near God!
I have made the Sovereign LORD
my shelter, and I will tell everyone
about the wonderful things
You do.**

PSALM 73:28

The Lord] will cover you with His feathers. He will shelter you with His wings. His faithful promises are your armor and protection (Psalm 91:4).

Those who live in the shelter of the Most High will find rest in the shadow of the Almighty. This I declare about the LORD: He alone is my refuge, my place of safety; He is my God, and I trust Him (Psalm 91:1–2).

As for me, how good it is to be near God! I have made the Sovereign Lord my shelter, and I will tell everyone about the wonderful things You do (Psalm 73:28).

Show me Your unfailing love in wonderful ways. By Your mighty power You rescue those who seek refuge from their enemies. Guard me as you would guard Your own eyes. Hide me in the shadow of Your wings (Psalm 17:7–8).

Listen to me, descendants of Jacob, all you who remain in Israel, I have cared for you since you were born. Yes, I carried you before you were born. I will be your God throughout your lifetime—until your hair is white with age. I made you, and I will care for you. I will carry you along and save you (Isaiah 46:3–4).

A NOTE FROM CANDACE

PROTECTED

Among their many great qualities, my mom and dad proved to be wonderful show-business parents precisely because they didn't care to be show-business parents. Their priority was to be Mom and Dad and raise four respectful kids. Robert and Barbara Cameron insisted that my brother, Kirk, and I (the two who enjoyed acting) be home for family dinner, do our chores, and live under the same rules as our sisters, Bridgette and Melissa, who didn't want careers in front of the camera. Curfews and dating boundaries were the same for everybody.

Since my dad was a teacher, Mom took Kirk and me to most of our auditions. She is an intentional person, and though she'd never anticipated having kids in "the industry," she was very careful to protect us. For example, she was always on set with me or Kirk (he was on the hit sitcom *Growing Pains*). In the event that our schedules overlapped, Mom made sure we were being looked after by someone *she* knew and trusted. She also got to know the other cast members as well as the crew.

I remember at auditions she'd walk in with us to get our lines and then immediately guide us into a hallway or a private corner. That way my brother and I could practice without feeling pressured. Mom's tactic also gave us kids more confidence in front of casting directors. Since we weren't caught up in comparing ourselves with the other auditioners, we were free to have fun and just do our best.

My mom's protective heart and style remind me of God, who promises to shelter us under His wings, like a mother bird with her babies. Mom shielded Kirk and me from things that might have hurt us or affected our mindset. She did it in such a way that we didn't have to worry. We belonged to her. We were safe under her wing—and we knew it.

God keeps all His kids under His wing. As an adult, I visualize myself in that place, close to His heart, all the time. It makes me feel protected and comforted. Sometimes He picks me up when I fall. Occasionally He has to nudge me forward, out of the nest, so I can stretch and fly. Mostly, though, I rest in knowing that I belong to Him, safe in His care.

THINK ON IT

When you recall feeling especially safe and intentionally protected, what memory comes to mind? Who looked out for you?

What actions do you take to protect your loved ones?

THINK ON IT

How do you visualize God shielding you so that you can release your worries or concerns?

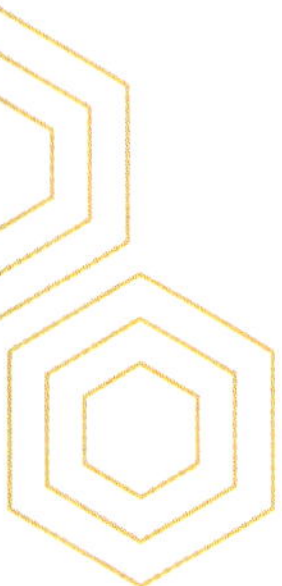

Of the several verses on the Scripture page, which one resonates the most with you? Why?

In what ways does God's shelter set you free and give you confidence that you wouldn't have otherwise? How can you put yourself under His wing in a current situation?

ACT ON IT

Psalm 73:28 is a beautiful verse:

> *As for me, how good it is to be near God! I have made the Sovereign Lord my shelter, and I will tell everyone about the wonderful things You do.*

Draw a picture of what being sheltered by God means to you, or write a story, song, or poem about it here. Or you could print out a photo and paper clip it to this page. Include the wonderful things He does that you would like to tell others about.

While you're doing this, listen to music that comforts you.

Pop on over for a video from me (Candace) on today's topic!

Heads Up!

Surely Your goodness
and unfailing love
will pursue me
all the days of my life,
and I will live in the house
of the LORD forever.

PSALM 23:6

I am the Alpha and the Omega—the beginning and the end," says the Lord God. "I am the one who is, who always was, and who is still to come—the Almighty One" (Revelation 1:8).

"My thoughts are nothing like your thoughts," says the LORD. "And My ways are far beyond anything you could imagine. For just as the heavens are higher than the earth, so My ways are higher than your ways and My thoughts higher than your thoughts" (Isaiah 55:8–9).

We think you ought to know, dear brothers and sisters, about the trouble we went through in the province of Asia. We were crushed and overwhelmed beyond our ability to endure, and we thought we would never live through it. In fact, we expected to die. But as a result, we stopped relying on ourselves and learned to rely only on God, who raises the dead. And He did rescue us from mortal danger, and He will rescue us again. We have placed our confidence in Him, and He will continue to rescue us. And you are helping us by praying for us. Then many people will give thanks because God has graciously answered so many prayers for our safety (II Corinthians 1:8–11).

Surely Your goodness and unfailing love will pursue me all the days of my life, and I will live in the house of the LORD forever (Psalm 23:6).

I trust [the Lord] with all my heart. He helps me, and my heart is filled with joy. I burst out in songs of thanksgiving (Psalm 28:7).

A NOTE FROM CANDACE

HEADS UP!

As much as we might pray for our dreams to come true, they don't always happen in the way we hoped or in the timeframe we hoped. What then?

Pastor Charles Stanley has said that in life, "disappointment is inevitable. But to become discouraged, there's a choice I make."* What's your response when things don't follow your plan? Do you worry even more? Become disheartened? Downgrade your expectations? Or do you "look up to . . . the LORD," your true help (Psalm 121:1–2), expecting an upgrade?

I'll take the upgrade, please. God may have another option besides my version of the vision. Something much better than what I've imagined. I want to keep my eyes and heart open to *that*.

A young man named William lived with this expectation. After William's first semester at a Christian college, the school's president predicted, "At best, all you could amount to would be a poor country . . . preacher somewhere out in the sticks." But the man also told William, "You have a voice that pulls. . . . God can use that voice of yours . . . mightily."

In 1937, the young man transferred to Florida Bible Institute, where he received his calling to ministry on the eighteenth green at a local country club. He intended to become a military chaplain, but a case of mumps kept him from that line of work. Following stints as a small-church pastor and a Christian college president, he found his purpose in public preaching events that he called "crusades." By the time William "Billy" Graham died in 2018, that going-nowhere preacher with the mighty voice had shared the gospel in person to more people than anyone in the history of Christianity, with an estimated two billion or more people being reached in every major language through his combined broadcasting, preaching, and publishing ventures.

As Graham's life illustrates, God's ways and ideas are higher than ours. That means His dreams and plans are greater than we even know. So when it comes to determining the best fulfillment of our dreams, well, that's up to Him. He is the Alpha and Omega, the Beginning and the End of everything, and we have to leave room for Him to be God, letting Him guide us down the path He chooses.

He may not move you "up" in the world's eyes. In fact, the Lord may draw you from a palace to a wilderness, like He did with Moses. Here's the good news: When God recasts your vision or reconfigures your route to success, it is because He has something far better in mind. Hold on, and keep your head up!

---

* https://excelnetwork.org/blog/2015/4/25/how-to-deal-with-the-big-d

THINK ON IT

Have you downgraded from disappointment to discouragement over a dream of yours? When did your disappointment make a downturn?

What's your biggest worry if God doesn't answer your prayers as you expect?

What if He does *give you your dream—but wrapped in a different package? That happens a lot. What are some other forms your heart's desire might take?*

THINK ON IT

We learn in Exodus 13 that on the Israelites' journey to the Promised Land, "God did not lead them along the main road that runs through Philistine territory, even though that was the shortest route to the Promised Land" (verse 17). He knew that if they faced enemy attacks so early on, which was likely on the direct route, they would choose the "safety" of slavery in Egypt over God's plan. "So God led them in a roundabout way through the wilderness toward the Red Sea. Thus the Israelites left Egypt like an army ready for battle" (verse 18). In your own life, can you think of one or more reasons why God may have diverted your path, as He did with the Israelites when they left Egypt?

Paul the apostle endured a slew of hardships, from shipwrecks to beatings to jail time, simply for preaching the gospel. Not what he had originally planned, yet when he looked up from his circumstances, he testified of victory: "I want you to know, my dear brothers and sisters, that everything that has happened to me here [in jail] has helped to spread the Good News. For everyone here, including the whole palace guard, knows that I am in chains because of Christ. And because of my imprisonment, most of the believers here have gained confidence and boldly speak God's message without fear" (Philippians 1:12–14). God's dreams extend beyond us. He longs to use us to inspire others and advance His kingdom. Look up and see: How is God doing that through you?

ACT ON IT

Ministry leader Sid Woodruff has identified four Ds that disappointment can lead to if we leave it unchecked*:

1. Discouragement
2. Doubting God
3. Departing from the Lord
4. Defeated Life

With all the demands on our time and energy and emotions as women, drawing sure boundary lines based on the priorities God has shown us is vital for our decision making and protection. Boundaries also serve as hedges against unnecessary worries and limiting anxieties.

For each of the four downgrades listed above, define the boundaries you need to set to protect yourself from going to those places. Write your boundaries around the edges of each box to symbolize your intent to remain on the lookout for something far better.

DISCOURAGEMENT

DOUBTING GOD

DEPARTING FROM THE LORD

DEFEATED LIFE

I fully expect and hope that I will never be ashamed, but that I will continue to be bold for Christ, as I have been in the past. And I trust that my life will bring honor to Christ, whether I live or die.

PHILIPPIANS 1:20

Pop on over for a video from me (Candace) on today's topic!

* Sid Woodruff, "When Your Dreams Don't Come True" sermon at First Missionary Church, Berne, IN (April 25, 2010).

Challenge Accepted!

In my distress
I prayed to the LORD,
and the LORD answered me
and set me free. The LORD is
for me, so I will have no fear.
What can mere people do to me?
Yes, the LORD is for me;
He will help me. I will look in
triumph at those who hate me.

PSALM 118:5–7

One day Jonathan said to his armor bearer, "Come on, let's go over to where the Philistines have their outpost. . . . Perhaps the LORD will help us, for nothing can hinder the LORD. He can win a battle whether he has many warriors or only a few!" (I Samuel 14:1, 6)

So many are saying, "God will never rescue Him!" But you, O LORD, are a shield around me; You are my glory, the one who holds my head high (Psalm 3:2–3).

If you need wisdom, ask our generous God, and He will give it to you. He will not rebuke you for asking. But when you ask Him, be sure that your faith is in God alone. Do not waver, for a person with divided loyalty is as unsettled as a wave of the sea that is blown and tossed by the wind (James 1:5–6).

In my distress I prayed to the Lord, and the Lord answered me and set me free. The Lord is for me, so I will have no fear. What can mere people do to me? Yes, the Lord is for me; He will help me. I will look in triumph at those who hate me (Psalm 118:5–7).

It is God who enables us, along with you, to stand firm for Christ. He has commissioned us, and He has identified us as His own by placing the Holy Spirit in our hearts as the first installment that guarantees everything He has promised us (II Corinthians 1:21–22).

A NOTE FROM CANDACE

CHALLENGE ACCEPTED!

Quick—what's your default answer when you're challenged?

When your critics say, "God will never rescue her . . ."

When haters scoff among themselves at your efforts: "What does she think she's doing? Does she actually think she can rebuild from that mess?"

When a member of your own family mocks your faith, telling you, "Are you still trying to maintain your integrity?"

In those moments of decision, is your instinctive response "Yes!" "No!" "Maybe . . ." or "Let me get back to you"?

What about when the Lord is moving you to try something new or take a risk that you're not sure you're ready for?

Friends, it is imperative that we operate from a position of yes in those times. That King Saul's son Jonathan responded, "Perhaps the LORD will help us" (1 Samuel 14:6) rather than "What if He doesn't?" is huge! Daniel's friends, who were facing death by fire, told the king who had sentenced them to the furnace, "The God whom we serve is able to save us" (Daniel 3:17).

Worriers start with no. Warriors assume it's a yes unless and until God says no. That's a night-and-day difference.

I've seen in my own life how *no* thinking causes me to play it safe. Demanding safety—insisting that I won't take a chance without a guarantee—removes God from the experience, which actually puts me at greater risk. The older I get, though, the less I want to play it safe. Because I'm discovering how trustworthy and good God is. He's just the kind of leader I want to follow, a guide I can be sure of.

The way I see it, a believer who will take risks in the Lord is way better off than an unbeliever living in their comfort zone. A yes to God means you'll be finding your confidence and strength in Him. That's where big things happen.

Once your yes combines with His? Fireworks! You'll never be the same. Neither will your faith.

Just by stepping out, just by your step of faith toward Him, you'll see Him like you've never seen Him before. Before you know it, you'll be experiencing what the psalmist sang about: "What mighty praise, O God, belongs to You in Zion. . . . You faithfully answer our prayers with awesome deeds, O God our savior. You are the hope of everyone on earth, even those who sail on distant seas" (Psalm 65:1, 5).

THINK ON IT

When was a time that you were challenged by God to do something new and different? How did you react at first? If you said yes to that challenge, what was the result? If you said no, what are your regrets?

When God's people were trying to rebuild Jerusalem from the ground up, they encountered a lot of opposition like this: "Sanballat was very angry when he learned that we were rebuilding the wall. He flew into a rage and mocked the Jews, saying in front of his friends and the Samarian army officers, 'What does this bunch of poor, feeble Jews think they're doing? . . . Do they actually think they can make something of stones from a rubbish heap—and charred ones at that?'" (Nehemiah 4:1–2).

Noah's neighbors undoubtedly laughed at him, too, for building an enormous, three-story ark just because God said so (Genesis 6:13–22). Nevertheless, "Noah did everything exactly as God had commanded him" (verse 22).

How much harder has it been for you to say yes to something when you knew people would mock or question you? Did you do it anyway?

THINK ON IT

Review James 1:5–6 on the Scripture page. List the assurances and requirements of saying yes to God.

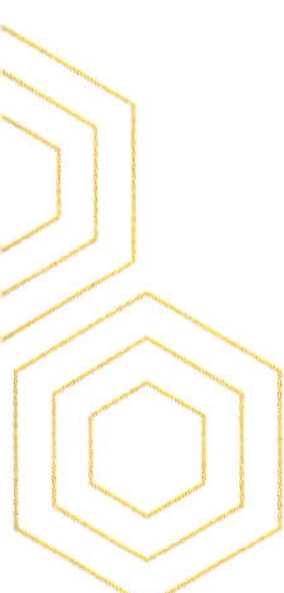

What kinds of divided loyalties can make people waver?
What divided loyalties sometimes cause you to waver?

Paul wrote in II Corinthians 1:19–20,
"Jesus Christ, the Son of God, does not waver between 'Yes' and 'No.' . . . As God's ultimate 'Yes,' He always does what He says. For all of God's promises have been fulfilled in Christ with a resounding 'Yes!'"
What does this good news do for your courage to step out in faith?

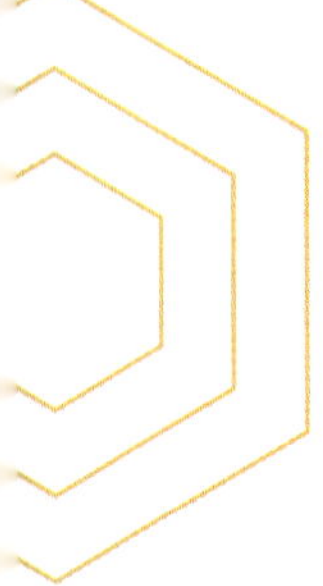

ACT ON IT

You know as well as I do: Taking up a God-given challenge doesn't ensure success. There's no promise that everything will go our way. Still, every warrior can say, "Yes, I accept! I will try!" That's a win right there. It lights a fire under you; at the same time, it sends a message that you're not playing—you're serious about fighting for the good God has in store for you.

What challenge has God been tugging at your heart to accept? Though it makes you uncomfortable or afraid, imagine yourself saying yes. How would you approach it differently if you committed to that answer? Live in that for five or ten minutes and then write down how it feels and what it would look like.

Now commit yourself to it! Say yes to God!

Questions and timidity usually come with the territory. This isn't any surprise to Him. So while you're at it, ask Him for everything you need: His courage, direction, and wisdom. Pray, "Lord, what's the first thing You want me to do?" However He guides you, no matter how out of character it might be, take the risk. Then ask Him to show you the next step and the next. He will walk you through it, all the way through. For anything He has called you to, you already have His answer: yes!

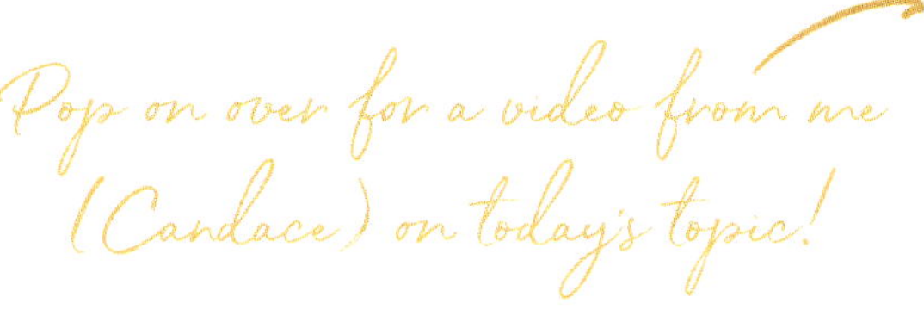

An Open Line

Always be joyful.
Never stop praying.
Be thankful in all circumstances,
for this is God's will for you
who belong to Christ Jesus.

I THESSALONIANS 5:16–18

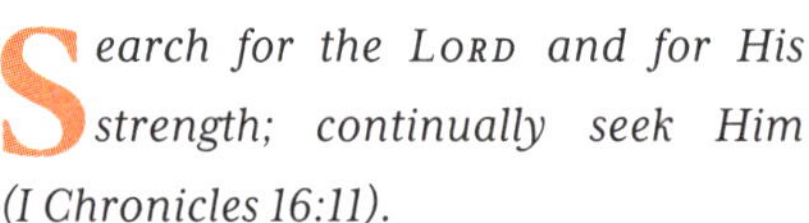

Search for the Lord and for His strength; continually seek Him (I Chronicles 16:11).

Always be joyful. Never stop praying. Be thankful in all circumstances, for this is God's will for you who belong to Christ Jesus (I Thessalonians 5:16–18).

Don't worry about anything; instead, pray about everything. Tell God what you need, and thank Him for all He has done. Then you will experience God's peace, which exceeds anything we can understand. His peace will guard your hearts and minds as you live in Christ Jesus (Philippians 4:6–7).

Dear brothers and sisters, we can boldly enter heaven's Most Holy Place because of the blood of Jesus. By His death, Jesus opened a new and life-giving way through the curtain into the Most Holy Place. And since we have a great High Priest who rules over God's house, let us go right into the presence of God with sincere hearts fully trusting Him. For our guilty consciences have been sprinkled with Christ's blood to make us clean, and our bodies have been washed with pure water (Hebrews 10:19–22).

[Jesus warned,] "When you pray, don't be like the hypocrites who love to pray publicly on street corners and in the synagogues where everyone can see them. I tell you the truth, that is all the reward they will ever get. But when you pray, go away by yourself, shut the door behind you, and pray to your Father in private. Then your Father, who sees everything, will reward you" (Matthew 6:5–6).

A NOTE FROM CANDACE

AN OPEN LINE

Maybe one reason we're told to "never stop praying" in I Thessalonians 5:17 is because God knew we would be bombarded with things to worry about. I doubt that any of us question the "pray" part, but it's easy to read this verse and wonder, *Is God literally saying, "Don't stop praying, ever"? Who can get anything done if He wants us praying all the time?*

In his book *A Word for the Day*, J. D. Watson confirms that the original Greek used in this verse means "without a gap."* But in Roman culture during biblical times, people would refer to someone with a nagging cough in the same way. It didn't mean "This person doesn't ever stop coughing for one second" but rather, "He or she keeps coughing."

That's how to pray: *keep* praying.

I look at this as keeping our communication lines with God open, to where we never actually end our call with Him.

Now, I'm somebody who felt very intimidated by this command for a long time. After all, prayer is talking to GOD (capital letters!), and I didn't grow up in church. Once I did become a Christian, every so often I'd come across one of those "professional" pray-ers. You know the type. The lofty ones who are super long-winded or switch to a new vocabulary as soon as they bow their heads. Hearing them made prayer seem even more daunting.

Mostly, though, I met a lot of sincere, positive people at church. They taught me that to pray with others and for others is simply an authentic conversation with God. He knows me inside and out, and He cares about me with the most tender heart possible.

With that perspective, suddenly you realize you can skip the big words and the long sentences. Talk like you would to someone who loves you.

Galatians 4:6 reminds us that "because we are His children, God has sent the Spirit of His Son into our hearts, prompting us to call out, 'Abba, Father.'" "Abba" is a heartfelt term of affection—more like "Daddy" than "Dad."

Our Daddy in heaven delights in hearing from His kids. You're not a nuisance to Him. He loves celebrating good news or savoring a special moment with you as much as He enjoys helping you process your specific thoughts, ideas, and concerns.

No need to pray about only the big stuff either. He knows where your keys are. You can go to God about whether to spend money on a "want" as confidently as you can about getting out of debt. He cares about you so seek Him first. After all, He has all the answers.

---

* Source: J. D. Watson, *A Word for the Day: Key Words from the New Testament* (Chattanooga, TN: AMG Publishers, 2006).

THINK ON IT

What do you love most about conversations with your best friend, your closest family member, or a caring mentor? How could you incorporate these "favorite things" into your conversations with God?

What hinders your prayers? Almost everybody feels blocked sometimes. Once you've identified those obstacles, prayerfully brainstorm some ways to get past those walls and include them here.

THINK ON IT

Like our conversations with others, our conversations with God will take different forms: requests for help, saying thank you, admiring His qualities, seeking His advice, asking for His forgiveness. They'll also vary in length. Simple words and simple sentences can be just as powerful as longer prayers. What are the benefits to having this flexibility?

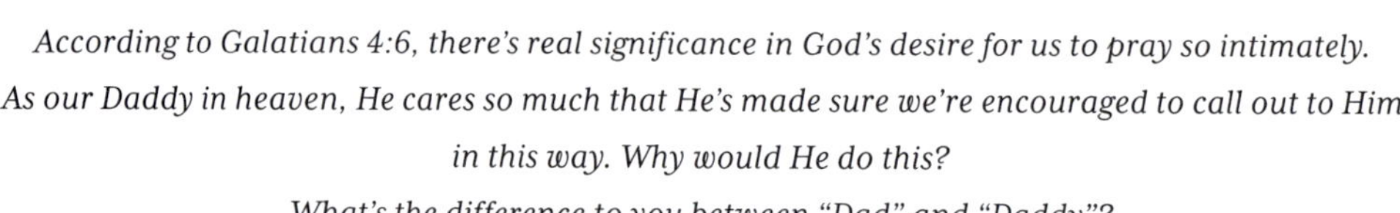

According to Galatians 4:6, there's real significance in God's desire for us to pray so intimately. As our Daddy in heaven, He cares so much that He's made sure we're encouraged to call out to Him in this way. Why would He do this?

What's the difference to you between "Dad" and "Daddy"?

What's something you could bring to your Daddy in prayer that you've never considered talking to Him about? Why don't you share that with Him now?

ACT ON IT

Without a doubt, making prayer a habit—setting aside time for God each morning and evening—is a great discipline. But let's keep Him on our minds and lips as we go through our day, too, knowing He's only a word, a sentence, a thought away. Sometimes prayer is simply saying "I trust You" as we're heading into a meeting, or "I'm sorry, Lord" when we realize we've done wrong, or "Give me strength" when we're feeling especially tired but need to stay on our game for another hour at work.

Think of some of the situations you consistently find yourself in that could benefit from prayer. List those in the left-hand column, and then, for the right-hand column, think of a word, a sentence, a phrase that would put your heart and mind in the right place for that moment.

MOMENTS I'D LIKE TO REMEMBER TO PRAY	A SIMPLE PRAYER FOR ME

I am praying to You because I know You will answer, O God.

PSALM 17:6

Pop on over for a video from me (Candace) on today's topic!

DAY 24

Cue the Music

I called on Your name, LORD,
from deep within the pit.
You heard me when I cried,
"Listen to my pleading!
Hear my cry for help!"
Yes, You came when I called;
You told me, "Do not fear."

LAMENTATIONS 3:55–57

Why am I discouraged? Why is my heart so sad? I will put my hope in God! I will praise Him again—my Savior and my God! Now I am deeply discouraged, but I will remember You. . . . I hear the tumult of the raging seas as Your waves and surging tides sweep over me. But each day the LORD pours His unfailing love upon me, and through each night I sing His songs, praying to God who gives me life (Psalm 42:5–8).

I called on Your name, LORD, from deep within the pit. You heard me when I cried, "Listen to my pleading! Hear my cry for help!" Yes, You came when I called; You told me, "Do not fear" (Lamentations 3:55–57).

You are my hiding place; You protect me from trouble. You surround me with songs of victory (Psalm 32:7).

Can anything ever separate us from Christ's love? Does it mean He no longer loves us if we have trouble or calamity, or are persecuted, or hungry, or destitute, or in danger, or threatened with death? . . . No, despite all these things, overwhelming victory is ours through Christ, who loved us (Romans 8:35, 37).

If God is for us, who can ever be against us? . . . Who dares accuse us whom God has chosen for His own? No one—for God Himself has given us right standing with Himself. Who then will condemn us? No one—for Christ Jesus died for us and was raised to life for us, and He is sitting in the place of honor at God's right hand, pleading for us (Romans 8:31, 33–34).

A NOTE FROM CANDACE

CUE THE MUSIC

In both television and the movies, you can count on the music being cued during sentimental or suspenseful moments. It elicits emotion and helps set the stage for what's to come.

Music is also a proven, and nearly instantaneous, stress reliever. Doctors have studied its effects on our heart rates, our brains, our moods—and music does our bodies good. It sure did for King Saul: "Whenever the tormenting spirit . . . troubled Saul, David would play the harp. Then Saul would feel better, and the tormenting spirit would go away" (I Samuel 16:23).

Christian comedienne Chonda Pierce found out firsthand just how true this is. She grew up a pastor's kid, and her descriptions of her childhood are hilarious. But this funny, funny lady has also endured some enormous trauma in her life. Several years ago, her depression grew so bad that Chonda couldn't pray for herself. She was seeing a therapist and taking prescription medications, and she had the support and prayers of trusted friends and family. Then she had the idea to put on some good music—praise and worship music to be exact—to keep her spirits up in her fight against the numbing darkness.

As she told *MTL (More to Life)* magazine, "Satan is the author of lies, and I've discovered that depression is his cell phone. He had me on speed dial, and he'd call me just to say that life is not worth living. . . . The good news is that he has a very limited calling plan, and my stereo is so much louder."*

She started playing praise music in her house to drown out the words of the enemy. She played it so loud, her own kids told her to turn it down! (Oh, how I love that!) She saw it this way: "If I didn't feel like praising, then the walls of my house could do it for me."*

For months, Chonda kept the music going, kept seeing her doctors, kept taking her meds. She also read Scripture, listened to the Bible on audio, lamented to God, and asked others to pray with her and for her. And gradually the heaviness began to lift.

If you just can't shake your anxiety or depression, don't feel like you have to go it alone. Be kind to yourself and seek out professional help along with spiritual support. I'd also urge you to do as Chonda did: Cue the music and turn up the volume. It will set the stage for your healing to come!

* Chonda Pierce, "Lessons from a Depressed Comedian," *MTL* (July/August 2006), 50–53.

THINK ON IT

What's your favorite "overcomer/fight" song?
Write out the lyrics from it that really inspire you.

Why are these words meaningful to you?

The prophet Jeremiah lamented: "The thought of my suffering and homelessness is bitter beyond words. I will never forget this awful time, as I grieve over my loss. Yet I still dare to hope when I remember this: The faithful love of the LORD never ends! His mercies never cease. . . . The LORD is good to those who depend on Him, to those who search for Him. So it is good to wait quietly for salvation from the LORD" (Lamentations 3:19–22, 25–26).
Where is the turning point in his words? When does his grief begin to shift?
How can you apply his example?

THINK ON IT

James the apostle wrote, "We give great honor to those who endure under suffering. For instance, you know about Job, a man of great endurance. You can see how the Lord was kind to him at the end, for the Lord is full of tenderness and mercy" (James 5:11).

Job is introduced in the Bible as "a man of complete integrity" who "feared God and stayed away from evil" (Job 1:1). Satan took nearly everything from—his children, his wealth, his property, his health.

Yet in Job's grief, he did not sin against God or curse the Lord's name.

And in the end, the Lord restored to him twice what the enemy had taken.

Who is your personal example of great endurance—from history, from the Bible, or from your own life?

"The Holy Spirit helps us in our weakness," wrote Paul. "For example, we don't know what God wants us to pray for. But the Holy Spirit prays for us with groanings that cannot be expressed in words. And the Father who knows all hearts knows what the Spirit is saying, for the Spirit pleads for us believers in harmony with God's own will" (Romans 8:26–27).

What comfort does this passage give you?

ACT ON IT

Music is such a fundamental and powerful force in our lives that it's nearly everywhere we go. Restaurants. Stores. At the gym. We listen to it at work and during our commutes and while we're doing chores. . . .

It's everywhere in the Bible too. Practically every book of Scripture has some reference to it. The final book, Revelation, is very clear that music will be a prominent part of life in heaven. Isn't that a relief? God doesn't expect us to ever live without it! So let's make it an integral part of our personal "stress-relief kit."

Take time to think about what should be in yours, but a good place to start would be to compile your favorite Scripture verses from this devotional guide and a praise song playlist. You might also include candles, a Bible, an inspiring book, a blanket, some bath bombs, warm socks, special teas, comfy clothes, and, of course, some chocolate. Put all those items in a pretty basket, and keep them handy for the next rainy day or difficult week.

Stress-Relief Kit

PRAISE SONG PLAYLIST

FAVORITE VERSES

Stay Out of the Sinkhole

You will keep in perfect peace
all who trust in You,
all whose thoughts
are fixed on You!
Trust in the LORD always,
for the LORD GOD
is the eternal Rock.

ISAIAH 26:3–4

God's truth stands firm like a foundation stone with this inscription: "The LORD knows those who are His," and "All who belong to the LORD must turn away from evil" (II Timothy 2:19).

You will keep in perfect peace all who trust in You, all whose thoughts are fixed on You! Trust in the LORD always, for the LORD GOD is the eternal Rock (Isaiah 26:3–4).

He alone is my rock and my salvation, my fortress where I will never be shaken (Psalm 62:2).

The LORD is my rock, my fortress, and my savior; my God is my rock, in whom I find protection. He is my shield, the power that saves me, and my place of safety (Psalm 18:2).

How can a young person stay pure? By obeying Your word. I have tried hard to find You—don't let me wander from Your commands. I have hidden Your word in my heart, that I might not sin against You. I praise You, O Lord; teach me Your decrees. . . . I have rejoiced in Your laws as much as in riches. I will study Your commandments and reflect on Your ways. I will delight in Your decrees and not forget Your word (Psalm 119:9–12, 14–16).

Anyone who listens to My teaching and follows it is wise, like a person who builds a house on solid rock. Though the rain comes in torrents and the floodwaters rise and the winds beat against that house, it won't collapse because it is built on bedrock. But anyone who hears My teaching and doesn't obey it is foolish, like a person who builds a house on sand. When the rains and floods come and the winds beat against that house, it will collapse with a mighty crash (Matthew 7:24–27).

A NOTE FROM CANDACE

STAY OUT OF THE SINKHOLE

When my hockey-playing husband was traded to the Florida Panthers in 2001, we bought a home near Fort Lauderdale, where we lived for several years. After braving Canada's cold while he played for NHL teams there, this California girl was thrilled (Tha-RILLED!) to be headed to the balmy, beachy Sunshine State.

But you know what they don't speak of in the real estate listings? The possibility of sinkholes. Florida has lots of them. More than anyplace in the US. And if you've ever caught sight of one on a Weather Channel special, you won't forget it. A sinkhole's ability to swallow up an entire house or neighborhood is almost surreal.

Worry can be a sinkhole too—starting small, and then, before we know it, swallowing us whole. But the Bible gives us many ways to remain on solid ground. Here are just a few:

Memorize Scripture. For more confidence when you don't have a Bible with you, try memorizing Scripture. If memorizing isn't your forte, make good use of Post-it notes and screen savers on your devices. No matter how we spend time with God's Word, the Holy Spirit is faithful to root it deep inside. I've seen this firsthand. I can't tell you the number of times God has brought some phrase or verse to mind in conversations or moments of stress. Storing up His Word in your mind is like stockpiling your kitchen pantry—only for your soul rather than your stomach. Keep a good supply of your favorite verses on hand and you'll never be without a word from God.

Change your focus. Are you fretting about something? As soon as you realize you're heading down that hole, divert your thoughts to something uplifting. Reflect on God's goodness to you. Sing a song that lightens your heart. Answer your worry with encouraging Scripture verses you've memorized. Flip through some of your favorite photos and videos in your phone albums. Or watch a show that makes you laugh.

Think outward. Get your mind off yourself and onto others. Who can you serve today? How can you help somebody else? Lightening someone else's load is a sure way to ease your own burden.

Limit your exposure. The attitudes or messages of others can expand your worry quickly. There's no sense in giving those people your ear in real life or online. Be selective about social media; steer clear of conversations that bring you down; and, as much as you can, surround yourself with loving, positive people.

Whatever you do, friends, don't stay passive! If you don't fight your way out, you'll keep sinking. Look to build your house on solid ground. Christ our Rock and the truths of His Word will never let you down.

THINK ON IT

Who or what in your life tends to expand your worry? How?

Who or what in your life helps ground you so that you worry less?

Reread the four passages from Isaiah and the Psalms on the Scripture page. What are the results of letting the Lord and His Word be your rock?

THINK ON IT

Romans 8:11–12 promises all Christians:
"The Spirit of God, who raised Jesus from the dead, lives in you. . . . Therefore, dear brothers and sisters, you have no obligation to do what your sinful nature urges you to do. . . . If through the power of the Spirit you put to death the deeds of your sinful nature, you will live."
Worry is one of the many struggles that arise from our sin nature. What aspects of your life in Christ empower you to avoid the sinkhole? How well are you using those truths to your advantage in the battle against worry?

What else would you add to the list from the devotional?

ACT ON IT

Worry is a slippery slope that can easily pull us farther and farther down, one thought at a time.

Think of a recent worry you had that landed you in a pit. At the mouth of the sinkhole on the left, write the initial worry that started it all. (Example: *My boss seemed irritated today.*) What was the thought that pulled you inside? List that next. (*Did I do something wrong?*) Keep going until you've catalogued your concerns in succession, all the way to the bottom. (*What if I messed up the report he asked for?* and so on . . .)

On the right, you see a ladder. Counter the spiraling thoughts you listed on the left with affirming, truthful thoughts that bring you out of the pit. (Examples: *Maybe my boss was simply tired . . . If I did make a mistake, I'll fix it . . . Let me ask if he is doing okay rather than making assumptions.*) Ultimately we want to stay out of the sinkhole entirely. Truthful thoughts are great for keeping our minds on solid ground.

THE SINKHOLE

TRUTHFUL THOUGHTS

Prepare your minds for action and exercise self-control.

I PETER 1:13

Pop on over for a video from me (Candace) on today's topic!

DAY 26

Even if I Fail

**My health may fail,
and my spirit
may grow weak,
but God remains
the strength of my heart;
He is mine forever.**

PSALM 73:26

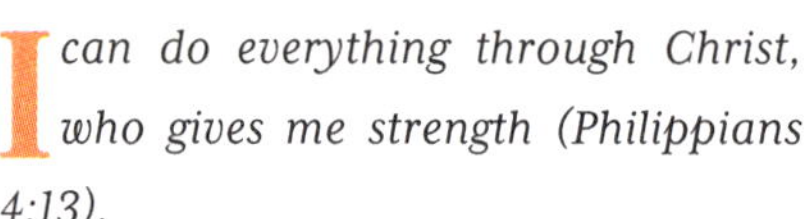

I can do everything through Christ, who gives me strength (Philippians 4:13).

Each time [the Lord] said, "My grace is all you need. My power works best in weakness." So now I am glad to boast about my weaknesses, so that the power of Christ can work through me. That's why I take pleasure in my weaknesses. . . . For when I am weak, then I am strong (II Corinthians 12:9–10).

I prayed to the Lord, and He answered me. He freed me from all my fears (Psalm 34:4).

God has not given us a spirit of fear and timidity, but of power, love, and self-discipline (II Timothy 1:7).

My health may fail, and my spirit may grow weak, but God remains the strength of my heart; He is mine forever (Psalm 73:26).

Be strong and courageous! Do not be afraid or discouraged. For the Lord your God is with you wherever you go (Joshua 1:9).

A NOTE FROM CANDACE

EVEN IF I FAIL

I can remember it like it was yesterday. I was about to head onstage for my first appearance on *Dancing with the Stars*, and I was so sick to my stomach that I was looking for the puke bucket. In the dressing room beforehand and while waiting in the wings with my dance partner, Mark Ballas, I had to keep telling myself, "God will give me strength even if I mess up. I am going to do it. He loves me, He loves me. The Lord is my strength . . ."

Being on *DWTS* got a little easier after that first night. Still, I was always really nervous as showtime approached. Failing is hard enough; failing in front of a live audience takes it to another level.

You know this because you have a live audience too. Yours might be your kids, your group of friends, your sorority, your coworkers, your church, or your clients. It's all the same: no one wants to face-plant in front of their people or falter in the opportunities God has provided.

Every time we put ourselves out there, the failure worries are likely to pop up. Thankfully, God offers the following reminders to you and to me and to every one of His daughters as we push past our fears and accept life's challenges:

- His love doesn't change based on your performance. He calls you to be obedient—that's your part. The results? That's His part.
- You can take your worry to the Warrior, knowing He will give you the words to say and the motivation and determination to do what He has called you to do. Having the confidence that He is with me and that He goes before me—walking ahead and preparing the way—is a mental picture I take with me into those nervous moments.
- Succeeding isn't the only way you improve. To try something you are scared of builds confidence too.
- God cultivates things in failure that might not grow deep roots otherwise, such as compassion toward those who fail us.

Of course there are times when I trust God, take the risk—and fail. It doesn't feel good to fail. That's the hard part. Yet I feel good because I trusted God. Remember failure is a matter of perspective. What we might see as failure, God can use for good.

Some days I have to step into the ring, in faith, before I can sense that the Lord is with me. Every time, though—there He is! Seeing Him show up in so many amazing ways, and in so many scenarios, has built my faith to expect Him to show up. I'm never sure how He'll do that, but I know He is always in my corner.

THINK ON IT

How recently have you taken a risk in spite of your worries? What was the situation?

Whether that experience was everything you dreamed or not what you hoped, where did you see God show up? How did that make you feel?

THINK ON IT

In what ways has a failure built up your confidence?

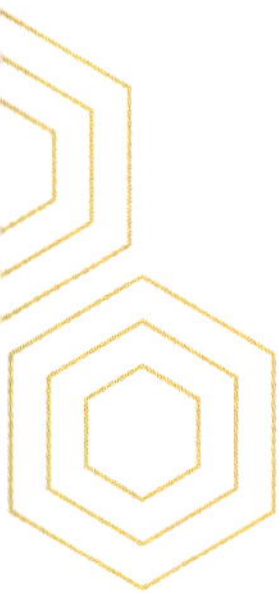

Reread the II Corinthians 12 verses on the Scripture page. When Paul writes, "When I am weak, then I am strong," what does he mean? Thanks to your growing relationship with God, what are you understanding about this truth that you never understood before?

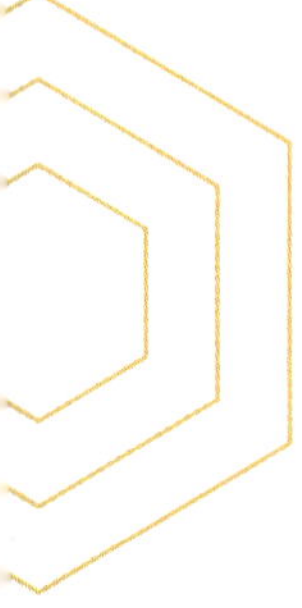

ACT ON IT

Make your own list of reminders to fend off worries of failure. What exactly has God taught you about pushing past your fears and taking on worthy challenges?

No Fear!

REMINDERS FOR MY CHALLENGES

Be strong and courageous! Do not be afraid or discouraged. For the LORD your God is with you wherever you go.

JOSHUA 1:9

Pop on over for a video from me (Candace) on today's topic!

DAY 27

Where Wisdom Begins

[Wisdom says,] "Joyful are those who listen to me, watching for me daily at my gates, waiting for me outside my home! For whoever finds me finds life and receives favor from the LORD. But those who miss me injure themselves. All who hate me love death."

(PROVERBS 8:34-36)

Charm is deceptive, and beauty does not last; but a woman who fears the LORD will be greatly praised (Proverbs 31:30).

Fear of the LORD teaches wisdom; humility precedes honor (Proverbs 15:33).

Gabriel appeared to [Mary] and said, "Greetings, favored woman! The Lord is with you! . . . Don't be afraid, . . . for you have found favor with God! You will conceive and give birth to a

son, and you will name Him Jesus. He will be very great and will be called the Son of the Most High. The Lord God will give Him the throne of His ancestor David. And He will reign over Israel forever; His Kingdom will never end!"

Mary asked the angel, "But how can this happen? I am a virgin."

The angel replied, "The Holy Spirit will come upon you, and the power of the Most High will overshadow you. So the baby to be born will be holy, and He will be called the Son of God. . . ."

Mary responded, "I am the Lord's servant. May everything you have said about me come true" (Luke 1:28, 30–35, 38).

[Wisdom says,] "Joyful are those who listen to me, watching for me daily at my gates, waiting for me outside my home! For whoever finds me finds life and receives favor from the L*ORD. But those who miss me injure themselves. All who hate me love death" (Proverbs 8:34–36).*

A NOTE FROM CANDACE

WHERE WISDOM BEGINS

If you've never read the last half of Proverbs 31, you need to check it out. It pictures a godly woman in action, making a difference through her business, her household management, and her care for others. Basically, it describes how effective we are and what a blessing we are to the Lord and to others.

However, within that passage is a phrase that can trip us up if it's misinterpreted: she "fears the LORD" (verse 30). Fearing God sounds like worry waiting to happen, doesn't it? I mean, who wants to serve someone you fear?

Biblically speaking, to fear the Lord means loving God through our reverence and our obedience. Honoring Him and hearing Him rather than pridefully acting like we know best.

For anyone who loves God, this holy type of fear doesn't heighten fear or increase worry. To the contrary, it actually lets you sleep better. Having peace is one of the rewards of following the Lord. What's more, it relieves you of many of the worries you would have otherwise—the kind of stuff that keeps people up at night when they're going around doing their own thing without one thought toward God.

"By fearing the LORD," says Proverbs 16:6, "people avoid evil." Not only that, as you obey Him "with deep reverence and fear," God works in you, "giving you the desire and the power to do what pleases Him" (Philippians 2:12–13).

Fearing God means you don't have to fear what Satan or any person might do. You have peace from a guilty conscience. Peace from the consequences of sin. Peace from peer pressure and the need to compromise to please others.

Having peace with God means you have peace, period.

When Mary was told she would give birth to God's Son, Jesus, she was confused and troubled at the announcement, as any virtuous woman would be. Once she learned that God would bring this about supernaturally, preserving her honor, she relaxed in obedience. Her response was, "I am the Lord's servant. May everything you have said about me come true" (Luke 1:38). In other words, "I'll trust You. Do as You please. Your wish is my wish."

When I read Mary's response and the song she sang in praise to God afterward (which we'll look at a little later), there's no resentment. She's not reluctant. It's a song of joy, of excitement, of anticipation. She wonders at—marvels at—what God is doing, but she is free of worry.

Like her, every God-fearing woman is beautiful. Every God-fearing woman can breathe and fulfill her calling. Most of all, every God-fearing woman is free to love God and love others with her entire being—just the way we love to love.

THINK ON IT

Does your view of God cause you to be afraid of Him? Afraid that He'll punish you for an honest mistake or that He is always disappointed in you? Or do you regard Him as Mary did? Why?

First Peter 1:18–19 explains an essential reason the Lord is worthy of our reverence: "For you know that God paid a ransom to save you from the empty life you inherited from your ancestors. And it was not paid with mere gold or silver, which lose their value. It was the precious blood of Christ, the sinless, spotless Lamb of God." What is so powerful about this? What are some other reasons you can think of?

THINK ON IT

The Bible highlights the incredible benefits of our reverence.
Beside each Scripture passage below, list the benefit in your own words:

- *"The Lord is a friend to those who fear Him. He teaches them His covenant" (Psalm 25:14).*
- *"Who are those who fear the Lord? He will show them the path they should choose" (Psalm 25:12).*
- *"You and your children and grandchildren must fear the Lord your God as long as you live. . . . Listen closely, Israel, and be careful to obey. Then all will go well with you" (Deuteronomy 6:2–3).*
- *The Lord is like a father to His children, tender and compassionate to those who fear Him" (Psalm 103:13).*
- *"The Lord watches over those who fear Him, those who rely on His unfailing love. He rescues them from death and keeps them alive in times of famine" (Psalm 33:18–19).*

ACT ON IT

To help us glimpse what's so beautiful about a heart that reverences God, look at Mary's answer to the angelic announcement and Mary's resulting song of praise (The Magnificat). This is that song, from the Gospel of Luke:

Oh, how my soul praises the Lord.
How my spirit rejoices in God my Savior!
For He took notice of His lowly servant girl,
and from now on all generations will call me blessed.
For the Mighty One is holy,
and He has done great things for me.
He shows mercy from generation to generation
to all who fear Him.
His mighty arm has done tremendous things!
He has scattered the proud and haughty ones.
He has brought down princes from their thrones
and exalted the humble.
He has filled the hungry with good things
and sent the rich away with empty hands.
He has helped His servant Israel
and remembered to be merciful.
For He made this promise to our ancestors,
to Abraham and his children forever."

(VERSES 1:46-55)

In the *Christian Mom's Idea Book*, author Ellen Banks Elwell cites three things Mary did when she heard what the Lord was about to do:

1. She praised God.
2. She acknowledged her humble state.
3. She built her life on God's plan.*

This is a good time to practice Mary's response. Think of a situation where God is calling you to a challenge or a task that is so big you can't possibly accomplish it yourself. View it as an opportunity instead of a thing to worry over. Through that lens, offer your response:

PRAISE GOD

What can you praise Him for as this opportunity unfolds?

ACKNOWLEDGE YOUR HUMBLE STATE

How would you describe yourself and what you anticipate God will do?

BUILD YOUR LIFE ON GOD'S PLAN

What do you need to give to God so that He can do all that He longs to do through you?
How can you entrust yourself to Him?

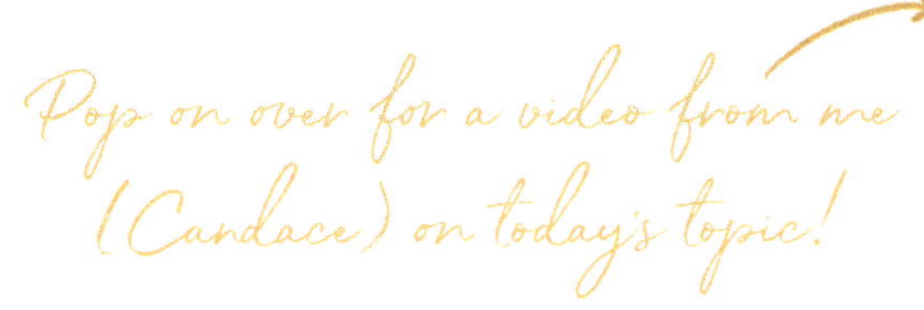

* Ellen Banks Elwell, *The Christian Mom's Idea Book: Hundreds of Ideas, Tips, and Activities to Help You Be a Great Mom* (Wheaton, IL: Crossway, 2008).

DAY 28

Work hard so you can present yourself to God and receive His approval. Be a good worker, one who does not need to be ashamed and who correctly explains the word of truth.

II TIMOTHY 2:15

Train yourself to be godly. "Physical training is good, but training for godliness is much better, promising benefits in this life and in the life to come" (I Timothy 4:7–8).

Don't you realize that in a race everyone runs, but only one person gets the prize? So run to win! All athletes are disciplined in their training. They do it to win a prize that will fade away, but we do it for an eternal prize (I Corinthians 9:24–25).

Be an example to all believers in what you say, in the way you live, in your love, your faith, and your purity. . . . Give your complete attention to these matters. Throw yourself into your tasks so that everyone will see your progress (I Timothy 4:12, 15).

Whatever you do, do well (Ecclesiastes 9:10).

Work hard so you can present yourself to God and receive His approval. Be a good worker, one who does not need to be ashamed and who correctly explains the word of truth (II Timothy 2:15).

Fight the good fight for the true faith. Hold tightly to the eternal life to which God has called you, which you have declared so well before many witnesses. . . . Then no one can find fault with you from now until our Lord Jesus Christ comes again (I Timothy 6:12, 14).

A NOTE FROM CANDACE

BOOT CAMP

Ever sign up for one of those fitness boot camps at your local gym? They're a "boot" all right—a kick in the pants that will get your booty (and the rest of your body) in shape.

Our Creator absolutely approves of physical training. Combine a good sweat with proper nutrition, sleep, and attention to your mental health, and you have the Great Physician's prescription for keeping your body strong.

God puts added value on spiritual training. Physical fitness is only for this life; spiritual fitness is for this life *and* the next. It helps us serve well, fight the good fight, finish our earthly race, and receive the eternal rewards that Christ made possible for all who put their faith in Him.

Faith training builds up both muscle and endurance: "Those who trust in the LORD will find new strength. They will soar high on wings like eagles. They will run and not grow weary. They will walk and not faint" (Isaiah 40:31). I definitely want those kinds of results! If I'm going to put in the time and effort to train, being able to reach new heights and run long distances without fainting sounds great!

So what is the Bible's training regimen for optimum performance? We need to know, because, like Team USA at the Olympics, no one in God's kingdom shoots for second place or trains for half the race. No.

We go for the gold. We run to win. We fight to the finish.

And while we fight hard, people are watching. They're looking to us as examples of perseverance and victorious, overcoming faith.

God's training plan includes great teammates—"Enjoy the companionship of those who call on the Lord with pure hearts" (II Timothy 2:22)—along with these exercises:

- "Keep in step with the Spirit" (Galatians 5:25 NIV).
- "Don't get sidetracked; keep your feet from following evil" (Proverbs 4:27).
- "Study [the Lord's] Book of Instruction continually" (Joshua 1:8).
- "Don't just listen to God's word. . . . Do what it says" (James 1:22).
- "Run from anything that stimulates youthful lusts. Instead, pursue righteous living, faithfulness, love, and peace" (II Timothy 2:22).
- "Trust in the LORD and do good" (Psalm 37:3).
- "Don't worry about the wicked or envy those who do wrong. For like grass, they soon fade away. Like spring flowers, they soon wither" (Psalm 37:1-2).

And finally, King Solomon challenges us to stay in our lane: "Look straight ahead, and fix your eyes on what lies before you. Mark out a straight path for your feet; stay on the safe path" (Proverbs 4:25-26).

We're in it to win it! So "let us strip off every weight that slows us down, especially the sin that so easily trips us up. And let us run with endurance the race God has set before us" (Hebrews 12:1).

THINK ON IT

What's your favorite type of exercise? What do you like about it?

What spiritual exercise do you enjoy most: Scripture memorization, listening to worship music, Bible study, listening to biblical teaching, prayer? How can you strengthen that practice? How can you strengthen one of the others?

THINK ON IT

"Cling to your faith in Christ, and keep your conscience clear," instructed the apostle Paul. "For some people have deliberately violated their consciences; as a result, their faith has been shipwrecked" (I Timothy 1:19). Those people lost their races due to compromise. They never crossed the finish line. Where are you compromising in your choices or behaviors that might cause you to stumble?

Proverbs 16:18 says, "Pride goes before destruction, and haughtiness before a fall." Examine your attitudes. Is there anything there that could keep you from crossing the finish line?

ACT ON IT

A good workout does wonders for the mind, body, and spirit. So let's shoot for some sort of physical and spiritual exercise three times a week for the next two weeks and see if that doesn't kick-start a staying-in-shape habit. The goal is to combine the two. For example, as you walk or jog or work out, work on memorizing a Bible verse. Or spend some time in prayer. Or listen to a devotional podcast, good worship music, or your favorite Christian teacher. Whatever helps you train your sights on God. Track your goals and your progress on the next page, and be sure to cheer for yourself each time you finish. Nothing wrong with a little pat on the back! You're a warrior. You've earned it!

Week 1

MY PHYSICAL EXERCISE GOAL ____________________

MY SPIRITUAL EXERCISE GOAL ____________________

	MY PHYSICAL WORKOUT	RESULTS (HOW DID I DO?)	MY SPIRITUAL WORKOUT	RESULTS (HOW DID I DO?)
WORKOUT #1				
WORKOUT #2				
WORKOUT #3				

HOW DID THIS WEEK FEEL? ____________________

WHAT CHANGES AM I SEEING PHYSICALLY? ____________________

WHAT CHANGES AM I SEEING SPIRITUALLY? ____________________

Week 2

MY PHYSICAL EXERCISE GOAL ____________________

MY SPIRITUAL EXERCISE GOAL ____________________

	MY PHYSICAL WORKOUT	RESULTS (HOW DID I DO?)	MY SPIRITUAL WORKOUT	RESULTS (HOW DID I DO?)
WORKOUT #1				
WORKOUT #2				
WORKOUT #3				

HOW DID THIS WEEK FEEL? ____________________

WHAT CHANGES AM I SEEING PHYSICALLY? ____________________

WHAT CHANGES AM I SEEING SPIRITUALLY? ____________________

Pop on over for a video from me (Candace) on today's topic!

Before You Leap

**When you go through deep waters,
I will be with you.
When you go through
rivers of difficulty,
you will not drown.
When you walk through
the fire of oppression,
you will not be burned up;
the flames will not consume you.**

ISAIAH 43:2

You need not be afraid of sudden disaster or the destruction that comes upon the wicked, for the LORD is your security. He will keep your foot from being caught in a trap (Proverbs 3:25–26).

Even when I walk through the darkest valley, I will not be afraid, for You are close beside me. . . . Surely Your goodness and unfailing love will pursue me all the days of my life (Psalm 23:4, 6).

Don't worry about tomorrow, for tomorrow will bring its own worries. Today's trouble is enough for today (Matthew 6:34).

"I know the plans I have for you," says the Lord. *"They are plans for good and not for disaster, to give you a future and a hope" (Jeremiah 29:11).*

Letting your sinful nature control your mind leads to death. But letting the Spirit control your mind leads to life and peace (Romans 8: 6).

When you go through deep waters, I will be with you. When you go through rivers of difficulty, you will not drown. When you walk through the fire of oppression, you will not be burned up; the flames will not consume you (Isaiah 43:2).

A NOTE FROM CANDACE

BEFORE YOU LEAP

I shared in my book *Kind Is the New Classy* about the time Whoopi Goldberg, my cohost on *The View*, came searching for me in my dressing room after I'd learned that a mass shooting had occurred not far from my son Lev's school. I was so distraught that when she found me, I was curled up in a closet, bawling my eyes out. And while it turned out that all the kids in Lev's school were safe, the fear of that day cut deep. I wasn't just worried; I was terrified, to the point of dread. I won't ever forget how awful the panic and helplessness felt.

You know as well as I do: We moms can go there in a heartbeat, and not only in emergency situations. Some of us jump from worry to worst-case scenario practically every day!

You don't have to have a child to make that leap either. Sometimes all it takes is a nudge in the direction of dread, and we're off and running.

Have you done that? Piled worry upon worry until it becomes the worst thing you can imagine?

Being the nurturing, intuitive souls that we are, we can often sense when something's up. It might be a little tension at work or church, a friend's casual comment, an odd reaction from our husband or boyfriend, our teenager's quietness . . . The radar goes off as soon as something's not right with our people.

This is the golden moment. I heard somewhere that, biologically, we have sixteen seconds to decide what we will do with a thought. We need to proceed with caution from here, so that our incredible capacity to tune in to others doesn't create a crisis.

If anybody understands our response in life's true 9-1-1 moments, it's God. After all, He equipped our bodies to pump adrenaline during emergencies. As His daughters, however, who are ruled by His Spirit, we shouldn't leap to catastrophic conclusions at the first trip of our radar. As we would with the motion sensors on our outdoor lights or an alert from one of our security apps, let's investigate before we assume the worst. Gather more information. Ask questions. And on those rare occasions when we do end up face-to-face with what we feared most, we can be confident that God has gone ahead of us. He's waiting there, and He's not about to let us go through it alone.

THINK ON IT

You receive an alert on your phone, a call from your child's school, or an email from your boss wanting to schedule a meeting. Where do your thoughts go first?

If you quickly jump to the extreme, what steps can you take to tame that instinct?

THINK ON IT

Psalm 112:4, 6–9 reads,
"Light shines in the darkness for the godly. . . . Such people will not be overcome by evil. . . .
They do not fear bad news; they confidently trust the LORD to care for them.
They are confident and fearless and can face their foes triumphantly.
They share freely and give generously to those in need. Their good deeds will be remembered forever.
They will have influence and honor."
What are the characteristics of godly people? How do these qualities aid us in preventing dread?

Reread the verses on the Scripture page. Which one should you commit to memory as a safeguard against automatically assuming the worst?

ACT ON IT

Emergency workers must train thoroughly and in advance for any situation. They don't have time to brush up on their skills when they arrive at an accident scene. We should similarly train our minds and hearts so that when we do face a crisis, we're prepared to handle it as people of faith, not as people without hope.

To combat dread in advance, business guru Dale Carnegie suggests asking yourself, "What is the worst that can happen?" and then mentally working out how you would deal with that situation.

Choose a worst-case scenario you worry about but that hasn't actually happened. Now process through it. What would you do? Who would you call? What resources would you need to have on hand? What would you want to tell yourself? How would you want to pray?

Once your action plan is in place, entrust this worry (and anyone it encompasses) to God.

WORST-CASE SCENARIO | ACTION PLAN

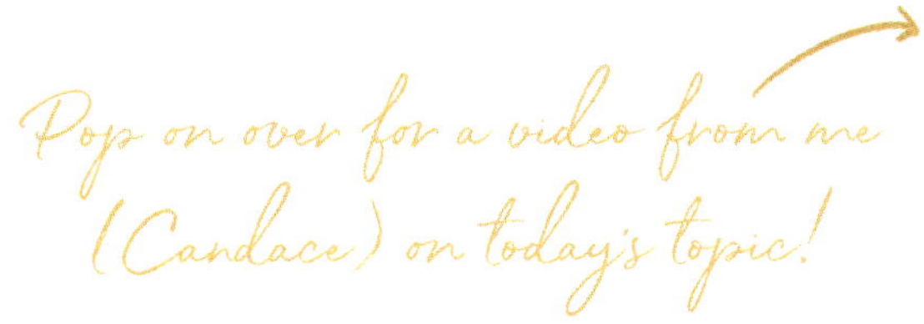

Priceless

All who are victorious will be clothed in white. I will never erase their names from the Book of Life, but I will announce before My Father and His angels that they are Mine.

REVELATION 3:5

Fire tests the purity of silver and gold, but the Lord tests the heart (Proverbs 17:3).

There is wonderful joy ahead, even though you must endure many trials for a little while. These trials will show that your faith is genuine. It is being tested as fire tests and purifies gold—though your faith is far more precious than mere gold. So when your faith remains strong through many trials, it will bring you much praise and glory and honor on the day when Jesus Christ is revealed to the whole world (I Peter 1:6–7).

Dear brothers and sisters, when troubles of any kind come your way, consider it an opportunity for great joy. For you know that when your faith is tested, your endurance has a chance to grow. So let it grow, for when your endurance is fully developed, you will be perfect and complete, needing nothing (James 1:2–4).

It is by [God the Father's] great mercy that we have been born again, because God raised Jesus Christ from the dead. Now we live with great expectation, and we have a priceless inheritance—an inheritance that is kept

in heaven for you, pure and undefiled, beyond the reach of change and decay (I Peter 1:3–4).

Think back on those early days when you first learned about Christ. Remember how you remained faithful even though it meant terrible suffering. . . . You knew there were better things waiting for you that will last forever. So do not throw away this confident trust in the Lord. Remember the great reward it brings you! (Hebrews 10:32, 34–35)

God blesses those who patiently endure testing and temptation. Afterward they will receive the crown of life that God has promised to those who love Him (James 1:12).

All who are victorious will be clothed in white. I will never erase their names from the Book of Life, but I will announce before My Father and His angels that they are Mine (Revelation 3:5).

Write this letter to the angel of the church in Philadelphia. . . . I know all the things you do, and I have opened a door for you that no one can close. You have little strength, yet you obeyed My word and did not deny Me (Revelation 3:7–8).

We are not like those who turn away from God to their own destruction. We are the faithful ones, whose souls will be saved (Hebrews 10:39).

A NOTE FROM CANDACE

PRICELESS

The Crown Jewels of the United Kingdom, housed at the Tower of London, are supposedly the most visited objects in the world. People are enamored with their history and their opulence, but what probably draws most visitors is the sheer beauty of these one-of-a-kind pieces.

The six-hundred-year-old collection of royal regalia includes two crowns. One of them is four and a half pounds of pure gold and semiprecious jewels and is worn only at coronations. The other is covered in diamonds and pearls and other rare jewels and is worn at formal occasions a few times each year.

If only those objects could speak! Every one of them would have a story to tell about how they got there.

The gold in those crowns had to be refined and purified by fire. The diamonds were formed deep in the dark earth under extreme heat and pressure. The pearls were created from the healing fluids of oysters layering over some irritant, such as a grain of sand, over months and months of time.

Nature's finest gems and precious metals originate in "suffering" circumstances. The most radiant have been through the hardest conditions. The most radiant are the most pure. And ultimately, they're the ones of greatest worth.

Just like us.

Do you sometimes wonder what God is doing through the pressures and pains of this life? He's transforming you into the Crown Jewels of heaven. He's producing diamonds from the rough. (The word *diamond* comes from a Greek word meaning "the invincible.") He's fashioning pearls of great price. Gold that glimmers. Not only that, but one day every jewel in His kingdom will be rewarded with crowns of her own.

I can't wait to see yours. I know many of you have taken anguishing, scary circumstances and, rather than turning ugly or being crushed as the enemy hoped, have grown in beauty, faith, purity, and character.

As Job did, you've decided to bless the name of the Lord rather than curse Him. Like Mary, and Paul, and David, and Esther, and Ruth, you've chosen to remain true to the Lord in spite of the worries and pressures of this life. Those are beautiful responses that only a woman of God can have. Those are the battle-tested responses of a warrior of God.

To endure the fire standing tall yet humble, strong yet vulnerable, brokenhearted yet open, injured yet forgiving, makes you as rare as they come, as true and truly lovely as can be. God sees your radiance as you live for Him. In His eyes, you are priceless. And one day, when you finally meet Jesus, your true Reward and Inheritance, you'll see what He sees. Then, you and I will be with Him forever. We'll rule with Him forever, the Crowned Jewels of His eternal kingdom.

THINK ON IT

What piece of jewelry do you prize the most, regardless of its monetary value? Or which jewel do you hope to own or inherit someday? Why? What does it symbolize to you?

List the spiritual riches that are part of our family inheritance from God, according to this passage: "God, the Father . . . has blessed us with every spiritual blessing in the heavenly realms because we are united with Christ. Even before He made the world, God loved us and chose us in Christ to be holy and without fault in His eyes. God decided in advance to adopt us into His own family by bringing us to Himself through Jesus Christ. This is what He wanted to do, and it gave Him great pleasure. So we praise God for the glorious grace He has poured out on us who belong to His dear Son. He is so rich in kindness and grace that He purchased our freedom with the blood of His Son and forgave our sins. He has showered His kindness on us, along with all wisdom and understanding" (Ephesians 1:3–8).

THINK ON IT

With the riches we receive from God, He wants us to build a faith that grows stronger under pressure and serve others in ways that count for eternity. Here's how Paul explained it: "No one can lay any foundation other than the one we already have—Jesus Christ. Anyone who builds on that foundation may use a variety of materials—gold, silver, jewels, wood, hay, or straw. But on the judgment day, fire will reveal what kind of work each builder has done. The fire will show if a person's work has any value. If the work survives, that builder will receive a reward" (I Corinthians 3:11–14). Which facets of your faith have grown stronger under pressure? What are you doing to serve others that will "survive the fire" and have eternal value?

The most beautiful part of every Christian's spiritual inheritance is this: "Then I saw a new heaven and a new earth, for the old heaven and the old earth had disappeared. . . . And I saw the holy city, the new Jerusalem, coming down from God out of heaven. . . . I heard a loud shout from the throne, saying, 'Look, God's home is now among His people! He will live with them, and they will be His people. God Himself will be with them. He will wipe every tear from their eyes, and there will be no more death or sorrow or crying or pain. All these things are gone forever.' And the one sitting on the throne said, 'Look, I am making everything new!' . . . He also said, 'It is finished! I am the Alpha and the Omega—the Beginning and the End. All who are victorious will inherit all these blessings, and I will be their God, and they will be My children' " (Revelation 21:1–7). What are you looking forward to the most on that day when God makes everything new?

ACT ON IT

The New Testament writers spoke of five crowns for believers. The godly will inherit one or more of these for faithfulness, love, and endurance on their life's journey.

Dr. David Jeremiah* explains each one:

1. The Victor's Crown is for those who continually, during their lives on earth, make disciplined choices with eternity in mind.
2. The Crown of Rejoicing, also known as the Soul-Winner's Crown, is given to those who share the gospel and reach others for Christ.
3. The Crown of Righteousness is for all who live aware that this world isn't their home and who anticipate Christ's return. They understand that eternal life with Him is their real reward.
4. The Crown of Glory will go to servant-leaders who, with integrity, answered God's call to minister to others through teaching, preaching, service, and administration.
5. The Crown of Life is given to believers who remain faithful to Christ through persecution and suffering. Some will end up giving their lives for His sake.

For your final Act On It, you decide what you'd like to do to represent what you're striving for as a warrior and a woman of God. Maybe create a crown that symbolizes one of the eternal crowns you hope to receive, constructing it with words, stickers, raw materials, cut-out or printed pictures, and colors that reveal your heart and your desire to live for the Lord. Or you could draw a multifaceted diamond or a string of pearls and on each segment write the enduring, beautiful qualities you'd like to cultivate.

Make it yours, and make it special. You are God's treasure.

Pop on over for a video from me (Candace) on today's topic!

* https://davidjeremiah.blog/what-kind-of-rewards-will-believers-receive-in-heaven/

Want more from Candace?
You can find her *One Step Closer Bible*, along with her series of Devotional Guides and inspirational gifts on dayspring.com, as well as several retail stores near you.

Dear Friend,

This Bible resource was prayerfully crafted with you in mind—it was thoughtfully written, designed, and packaged to encourage you right where you are. At DaySpring Bibles, our vision is to see every person experience the life-changing message of God's love, not just on Sundays, but every day of the week. As we worked through rough drafts, design changes, edits and details, we prayed for you to encounter His unfailing love and indescribable peace within the pages of this book. It is our hope that this resource doesn't only fill your head with knowledge, but strengthens your connection with and understanding of God.

THE DAYSPRING BIBLE TEAM

First Edition, August 2021

Published by:

21154 Highway 16 East
Siloam Springs, AR 72761
dayspring.com

Additional content collaboration provided by: Kris Bearss
Cover Design by: Brady Voss

Printed in United States
Prime: J6747
ISBN: 978-1-64870-285-3